WE PROTEST

The Public Order Debate

Peter Thornton

National Council for Civil Liberties

National Council for Civil Liberties
21 Tabard Street, London SE1 4LA

© Peter Thornton 1985

British Library Cataloguing in Publication Data

Thornton, Peter, *1946-*
    We protest: the public order debate.
    1. Great Britain, *Home Office.* Review of the
    Public Order Act 1936 and related legislation
    2. Great Britain. Public Order Act 1936
    3. Breach of the peace – Great Britain
    I. Title   II. National Council for Civil Liberties
    344.014'53

ISBN 0-946088-21-7

Phototypeset, printed and bound in Great Britain by
Yale Press Limited, London SE25 5LY

CONTENTS

1. INTRODUCTION

1.1 1985 is the year of the public order debate. In the past year several items of news have brought the issue of public order into sharp focus:- mass trials of striking miners, violence at football matches, the assault on the 'peace convoy' near Stonehenge, growing attendance at peace rallies, a secret manual of police tactics, road blocks to halt demonstrators, media hysteria about hooliganism and outbreaks of inner city disorder from Handsworth to Tottenham. This is the context of the debate in which a new Public Order Bill will be presented to Parliament. The real question will be: should the police be given sweeping new powers or has the law already moved too far from the protection of basic rights of protest?

1.2 The Government answers this question in a White Paper entitled 'Review of Public Order Law'[1], by calling for a considerable extension of police powers in the whole area of public order law – affecting marches, processions, meetings, static demonstrations, and criminal offences. In this paper the National Council for Civil Liberties (NCCL) sets out to redress the balance by providing not only a detailed critique of the Government's proposals, but also a clear alternative approach founded on the need to protect fundamental freedoms.

This paper is based on NCCL's submissions to the Home Office in response to the White Paper, which was prepared thanks to the speedy, hard work of a working party and decisions made by NCCL's Executive Committee.

1.3 The National Council for Civil Liberties was founded in 1934 to defend civil and political rights such as freedom of speech and assembly. The need to establish an independent watchdog organisation had resulted from the observation of police handling of the hunger marches in 1932.

In February 1934 Ronald Kidd, NCCL's first General Secretary, summoned to the crypt of St. Martin's-in-the-Fields twenty-five sympathisers – amongst them Harold Laski, Vera Brittain, Kingsley Martin, Edith Summerskill and Claud Cockburn – who joined the first Executive Committee, and elected E.M. Forster as NCCL's first President. One week later the first 'vigilance committee', independent observers charged with reporting on the behaviour of the hunger marchers and the police, gathered in Hyde Park at a meeting of unemployed workers, who, in the words of Kidd, were exercising 'the age-old liberty of the subject to demonstrate on an empty stomach'.

1

1.4 For the last fifty years NCCL[2], a non-party, non-denominational voluntary organisation, has continued to send independent observers to marches, demonstrations and public meetings. It has defended many charged with public order offences and taken up test cases on important public order issues.[3] Since its foundation NCCL has had two central concerns: first, that the right to peaceful assembly and peaceful protest should be upheld, and secondly, that the limits of the criminal law should be clearly, and narrowly, defined. It is with these concerns at the forefront of our consideration that we set out our criticisms of the Government's proposals and our alternative approach to the public order debate.

1.5 It is now nearly fifty years since the Government of the day hurried through legislation in response to the increasingly serious clashes between fascists and anti-fascists which culminated in the battle of Cable Street in October 1936. The Public Order Act of that year introduced curbs on processions and restrictions on uniforms and para-military organisations.

NCCL stressed then in its briefings to Members of Parliament that the new powers to ban processions were both unnecessary and undesirable. They were unnecessary because the Metropolitan Police Act 1839 already allowed the police to re-route processions – a power they failed to use in October 1936 until an hour or so after serious fighting had broken out in the East End. And undesirable because the Bill effectively ended 'the right to organise processions without the previous consent of the Executive', and left peaceful protestors vulnerable to bans imposed on the 'flimsiest of grounds'.

1.6 Fifty years on, the context and the arguments seem familiar. Bans have become commonplace, affecting thousands of trade union, nuclear disarmament and other peaceful protestors. Now further restrictions are proposed. Although there have been many discussion documents and submissions which led up to this White Paper, there is an air of undue political haste surrounding the timing of its publication. Comments on a number of key issues were requested by the Home Office to be given in under eight weeks. Widely differing issues – the miners' strike, football hooliganism, racist marches, peace rallies – have been gathered together under one heading, 'public disorder'. In the rush, rights have been confused with disorder; preventing disorder has developed into keeping the public in order. The pattern of hurrying through important legislation may be repeated: the Official Secrets Act 1911, the Public Order Act 1936, the Prevention of Terrorism Act 1974.[4] And now the Public Order Act 1985?

2. THE GOVERNMENT'S APPROACH

2.1 In June 1979 the Home Secretary announced a public order review following the disturbances at Southall in April of that year. The White Paper called *Review of Public Order Law*[1] was presented to Parliament in May 1985. It sets out the conclusions of the review. The White Paper takes particular notice of the following reports: The Green Paper of 1980[2], the Home Affairs Committee Report of 1980[3], the Law Commission's Working Paper[4] and subsequent report[5] on Offences Relating to Public Order and Lord Scarman's reports on the Red Lion Square Disorder[6] and the Brixton Disorder[7].

2.2 The White Paper is an extensive, but by no means comprehensive review of existing public order law. Although it proposes to abolish the ancient common law offences of riot, rout, unlawful asembly and affray, it proposes to replace them with the creation of new statutory offences of riot, violent disorder, affray and disorderly conduct, along with the extension of the much criticised offence of threatening, insulting, abusive words and behaviour etc. (Section 5, Public Order Act 1936). Four further new offences will be created for various forms of failing to comply with police requirements which will be accompanied by corresponding new arrest powers.

New controls will be placed on marches and processions. Notice must be given to the police of an intended march or procession at least seven days in advance. Non-compliance may lead to prosecution. The police power to impose conditions on marches and processions will be extended by adding to the test of the likelihood of serious public disorder the further tests of serious disruption to the local community or the coercion of individuals. For the first time similar powers will be granted to the police to control static demonstrations, including open-air meetings, assemblies and pickets.

Consideration is being given to the introduction of a power to enable a police authority to recover policing costs from the organisers of demonstrations.

The law of incitement to racial hatred is to be amplified and a new offence of possessing racially inflammatory material is proposed.

2.3 As we have already indicated, the context provided by the

3

White Paper is a contrived climate of public disorder, made to appear more sinister and threatening than it is in reality. *NCCL makes a number of general criticisms of the Government's approach.*

First, the White Paper *fails to start from the correct standpoint.* Instead of identifying the existence of fundamental rights, the need for their protection and the principle that only minimum restrictions should be placed on them, the White Paper is wholly concerned with the avoidance of public disorder and inconvenience. Its underlying concept is not to protect established rights, but to keep the peace, and in doing so it savagely undermines the basic freedom of peaceful assembly and protest. Violence and intimidatory behaviour must be condemned, but the White Paper manages to equate protest with disorder, an inconvenient privilege which must be controlled, restricted and avoided where possible. Thus it lumps together animal rights protests, National Front marches, peace protests, football hooliganism and mass picketing. Yet the conduct and context of these events differs greatly. For example, the Metropolitan Police Commissioner's report for 1983 (page 49) makes a clear distinction between the co-operation and peaceful nature of demonstrations organised by CND, and the disorder during demonstrations by various animal rights organisations.

2.4 Secondly, the White Paper *fails to provide any legal framework* for the fundamental right of peaceful assembly, including the right to picket peacefully. In the absence of a constitutional framework or the incorporation of the European Convention of Human Rights into the law, protective legislation is urgently required to stem the steady erosion by judicial decision and Act of Parliament of the principle of public expression.

Freedom of assembly serves a vital function in democracy. In their different and varied forms, demonstrations serve to bring issues and grievances to the attention of the public, the media and the authorities. They permit a form of open, public communication not offered by the media, and allow protestors to create and affirm solidarity with one another. Therefore, freedom of assembly should be subject to the minimum restrictions necessary to avoid immediate physical harm to persons and their property. The use of the streets, highways and public places for demonstrations must be preserved. While recognising the importance of freedom of assembly[8] the White Paper then proceeds to undermine it. New powers for the police to decide on the duration, numbers and place of static demonstrations and to insist on prior notice of marches will render the right to demonstrate a hollow one and have a chilling effect on organisers of demonstrations as well as inhibiting the citizen from participating in them.

2.5 Thirdly, the White Paper *fails to recommend codification of Public Order law*. Its proposals are concerned with a number of important aspects, but its conclusion that there is no need for codification of public order powers is wrong. This conclusion is not justified by the White Paper's argument that there is advantage in the flexibility of common law powers which are defined and controlled by the courts, and the police have not sought codification and see no benefit in it.[9] The police see no benefit in codification because the courts are only too willing to uphold the wide exercise of police discretion[10] and to extend the scope of police discretion over ever larger and vaguer areas. Existing public order law is to be found, with difficulty, in a mass of outdated common law decisions, Acts of Parliament and local byelaws. Even Moriarty's police manual[11] and Stone's *Justices' Manual* used to proclaim a statutory power of arrest for the offence of obstructing a police officer in the execution of his duty. The police often used this 'power of arrest' where none actually existed for this particular offence. NCCL therefore takes the view that there is an urgent need for clarification by codification in order to make the rights, powers and duties better known and understood.

2.6 Fourthly, the White Paper *fails to consider the causes of public disorder*. This is a glaring omission. It sees public order and disorder as clearly defined states requiring no analysis. This lack of inquiry into the reasons for disorder quickly dispels any illusion of concern for balance in the White Paper. It is replaced by a vigorous attack upon the freedom of people to gather together in numbers. Very few gatherings lead to violence. The White Paper refers to seventeen incidents of major disorder in London between 1974 and 1981. But it fails to consider whether the exercise of police powers is itself a major cause of disorder. The worst disorder in London – in Brixton in 1981 – was a reaction to police behaviour[12] and could not have been prevented by the new powers proposed by the White Paper. Similar reaction in 1985 has caused widespread inner city tension to erupt on the streets. In the USA the Kerner Commission on civil disorder[13] found that police behaviour was the most frequently perceived source of grievance in the black community. In view of the substantial escalation of disorder which has been known to occur where the police have attempted to make arrests in the presence of large numbers of people (recent events near Stonehenge provided a graphic example), it is surprising that so much emphasis should be placed on creating powers for the police, particularly powers to arrest people who are not behaving in a disorderly way and whose behaviour may be motivated only by a strong desire to demonstrate peacefully without interference.

2.7 Fifthly, the White Paper proposes *an unnecessary and undesirable extension of police powers*. The existing law provides more than enough scope for controlling disorder. Although the Public Order Act 1936 is considered to be the central plank of public order law, those who control public order and disorder have many equally powerful planks at their disposal. The police have extensive common law and statutory coercive and arrest powers to prevent disorder and the obstruction of the highway (see Chapter 4 below). Local byelaws and local Acts of Parliament give additional powers to police and local authorities to restrict and control processions, assemblies and meetings, and a full range of criminal charges provides penalties from small fines to lengthy terms of imprisonment. The new powers will dramatically curb existing freedoms, such as they are. They will infringe upon lawful activity and will put innocent demonstrators at risk of prosecution. It should be noted that the course adopted is consistent with the sweeping new police powers, including 96-hour detention, passed recently in the Police and Criminal Evidence Act 1984.

2.8 Sixthly, the White Paper's proposals will also *defeat the very purposes of the review: the prevention of disorder*. The greater use of banning orders, restrictions and conditions, powers of arrest and criminal charges will inevitably create resentment and hostility towards the police. Where there has been co-operation there will now be confrontation. The recent pledge by Sir Kenneth Newman, Commissioner of the Metropolitan Police, to authorise the use of plastic bullets and CS gas, imported from Northern Ireland, will similarly exacerbate, not quell violence. The Government has succumbed to the temptation to say that where a specific power has failed (as with the riot cases) there is something wrong with the power and it should therefore be strengthened. They fail to see that either the wrong power is being used or that the power is ineffective because it is unacceptably widely defined.

2.9 NCCL therefore *recommends* that:

(i)   The law relating to public order should be codified.
(ii) The overall approach to codification should be founded on the need to protect fundamental freedoms; and should have as its secondary purpose the prevention of public disorder.
(iii) The structure of the code should seek to:

- enshrine the right of peaceful assembly, including the right of peaceful picketing

- emphasise the need for co-operation with the police and local authorities in the exercise of these rights

- amend the law relating to the use of the highway

- provide for basic police coercive powers

- restrict the number of public order offences

- rely on the use of specific assault, criminal damage and offensive weapon charges

- base coercive powers and criminal charges upon a clear public disorder test of the actual use of violence or immediate threats of violence to persons and property

- extend the law on incitement to racial hatred

- provide minimum restrictions by way of bans and conditions on marches and procession, together with an effective right of appeal

  (iv) The majority of the proposals in the White Paper should be rejected as inconsistent with this approach. Many of the specific proposals, dealing in particular with the creation of new offences, new arrest powers, new powers to control all types of assembly, are unacceptable to a free and democratic society. Unnecessary and undesirable, they will lead to restraints on the basic freedoms of peaceful assembly and free speech and will inevitably lead to an increase in violent confrontation with the police and other breaches of the law.

A summary of NCCL's detailed proposals is set out in Chapter 16 below.

3. POSITIVE RIGHTS

3.1 *Lip service* is undoubtedly paid to the importance of the principles at issue in the review

- 'the rights of peaceful protest and assembly are amongst our fundamental freedoms: they are numbered among the touchstones which distinguish a free society from a totalitarian one.' (White Paper para 1.7)

- 'The review has as its starting point the need to safeguard certain fundamental human rights – the rights of peaceful assembly and public protest and the right to public order and tranquility.' (Green Paper para 12)

- 'We said that this area of the law is closely connected with the exercise of fundamental liberties of the subject and that in such an area it was necessary to move with caution in considering the ambit of any new offences.' (Law Commission No. 123 para 2.2)

But once articulated, these principles are quickly relegated to second place. The Green Paper allocated some space to considering a statutory right to demonstrate, but with little enthusiasm. The White Paper briefly mentions balancing freedoms, but concludes: 'The Government has been concerned in the review to ensure that the law provides the police with adequate powers to deal with disorder, or where possible to prevent it before it occurs, in order to protect the rights and freedoms of the wider community.'[1] The balancing act see-saws under the weight of protecting 'the wider community'. Thereafter the White Paper gives little weight to positive rights, particularly those of which the 'narrower' community might wish to take advantage.

3.2 NCCL therefore *recommends* that *a statutory right to demonstrate should be enacted*. Its absence is lamentable; the arguments in favour of it are overwhelming.

(i) The existence of any form of right of assembly under the common law is uncertain in both nature and extent. From time to time judges either as legal arbiters (such as Lord Denning in his dissenting judgment in *Hubbard v Pitt*[2]) or as prominent figures (such as Lord Scarman in his Red Lion Square Report[3]) have referred publicly to the existence of fundamental rights and in particular to the rights of peaceful assembly and public protest. But if such rights do exist under the common law they do so purely in the negative sense. Demonstrations are not lawful because the law recognises the right of assembly; they are lawful only when and if they infringe no other law. The common law only permits that which is not forbidden.

A more usual approach to these issues can be seen in the opening words of Lord Chief Justice Hewart's judgment in *Duncan v Jones*[4], a case concerning the right of an unemployed worker to speak at a public meeting:

> 'There have been moments during the argument in this case when it appeared to be suggested that the Court had to do with a grave case involving what is called the right of public meeting. I say 'called', because English law does not recognise any special right of public meeting for political or other purposes. The right of assembly, as Professor Dicey puts it, is nothing more than a view taken by the Court of the individual liberty of the subject.'

(ii) The very content of the Government White Paper shows that the right of assembly, such as it is, is inadequately protected. The common law, through the judges, has constantly eroded basic civil liberty principles. Decision after decision has frustrated the exercise of rights, not protected them: *Duncan v Jones*[5] on free speech and assembly; *Piddington v Bates*[6], *Thomas & Ors v National Union of Mineworkers (South Wales Area)*[7] and *Waite v Taylor*[8] on picketing and the use of the highway; *Hubbard v Pitt*[9] on consumer picketing; *Moss v McLaughlan*[10] and the Dartford Tunnel case[11] on freedom of movement.

(iii) The positive value, if any, of any rights under the common law is completely undermined by the undue prominence which the law gives to the right of passage along the highway. Hence the use of the highway for peaceful protest is not lawful because it is a right, but only because of the negative reason that there has been no obstruction of the highway in the particular case. Furthermore, the offence of obstruction of the highway has been so developed and extended by judicial decision that its current meaning is far removed from its original purpose (see para 3.15 below). The balance, which Lord Scarman said had to be stressed to 'accommodate the exercise of the right to protest within a framework of public order which enables ordinary citizens, who are not protesting, to go about their business and pleasure without obstruction or inconvenience'[12], has been tilted away from the traditionally cherished freedom.

(iv) The enactment of statutory rights would have a positive effect. It would give priority under the law ('preferred status' in the USA) to the rights enacted, and put principle before exception. At present the exceptions, such as the offences of obstruction of the highway and obstruction of a police officer in the execution of his duty, are given priority.

3.3 What are the arguments against the enactment of positive rights?

First comes the broad philosophical approach, which prefers the flexibility of the common law and its tradition of permitting that which is not forbidden. The difficulty with this approach is that the development of the law is left almost entirely to the judges. They decide where the boundaries of rights should be. Unfortunately the judges have a pitiful record on the protection of rights, and the overwhelming tendency during the last century has been a general increase in legal restrictions on liberty.

Secondly, it is argued that the freedom to demonstrate is adequately recognised under existing law and needs no further protection. As we have argued above this is clearly not so.

Thirdly, it is said that the enactment of a general right under the law (as distinct from a specific and precisely defined right, such as a right of appeal) would be a novel and uncharted step. Such an enactment would certainly be unusual, although not unique. The right to protest has, for example, been variously described by Acts of Parliament (albeit by way of immunity not right, and therefore in a negative sense), and if the momentum of opinion on freedom of information and the right to privacy continues these principles will undoubtedly be enshrined in statute form in due course. There is no tenet of English law to prevent it, only the will of Parliamant.

Fourthly, it is argued that the right of assembly is not an absolute right and therefore any parliamentary definition will be capable of restriction by interpretation in the courts. There is undoubtedly some force in this argument. Not only will the precise formulation of the right be difficult, but the judges will delight in fettering the right by interpretation. Constitutional issues are the prerogative of the courts, they will say, not Parliament. The answer to this must lie with the positive advantages of statutory rights. It is high time that Parliament gave priority to positive rights. It is not enough to say that the judges will attack the scope of positive rights. If the courts diminish their force Parliament must strike again to amend the inadequacies.

3.4 How should the first positive right, *the right of assembly,* be defined?

As we have indicated above this task should be approached with caution. The presumption of liberty can all too easily be restrained by exceptions. The European Convention on Human Rights (1950) is a classic example of a document more enshrined in provisos than principle. The United Kingdom is a party to the Convention (as well as a frequent defendant in charges brought under it), and many wish to see its terms incorporated into English law. But Article 11 on freedom of assembly provides a clear example of the dangers of too broadly drafted exceptions. It provides:

1. Everyone has the right to freedom of peaceful assembly and to freedom of association with others including the right to form and to join trade unions for the protection of his interests.

2. No restriction should be placed on the exercise of these rights other than such as are prescribed by law and are necessary in a democratic society in the interests of national security or public safety, for the prevention of disorder or crime, for the protection of health or morals, or for the protection of the rights and freedoms of others. This Article shall not prevent the imposition of lawful restrictions on the exercise of these rights by members of the armed forces, of the police, or of the administration of the State.

3.5 There are other precedents.
The Universal Declaration of Human Rights (1948):

'Everyone has the right to freedom of peaceful assembly and association.'

The American Declaration of the Rights and Duties of Man (1948):

'Every person has the right to assemble peaceably with others in a formal public meeting or an informal gathering, in connection with matters of common interest of any nature.'

The International Covenant on Civil and Political Rights (1966):

'The right of peaceful assembly shall be recognised. No restrictions may be placed on the exercise of this right other than those imposed in conformity with the law and which are necessary in a democratic society in the interests of national security or public safety, public order, the protection of public health or morals or the protection of the rights and freedoms of others.'

3.6 NCCL *proposes* a definition on the following lines:

1. It shall be lawful for any person to be upon any highway or in or upon any public place for the primary purpose of peacefully expressing or communicating views.
2. It shall be a defence to any civil or criminal proceedings for a person to be acting reasonably in pursuance of this.

In putting forward this definition NCCL would welcome further discussion on the subject. It should be noted that the words 'to be upon' embrace marches, processions, meetings and pickets. The word 'primary' is used to exclude the misuse of the right, for example by traders seeking the protection of the Section by pretending to express or communicate views.

In our discussions we rejected an unnecessary and too narrow qualification upon 'views' that they should be 'upon issues of public concern and interest' (issues of private or individual concern should not be excluded) and a non-exhaustive list of issues, phrased as –

'For the purpose of this Section issues of public concern and interest shall include all issues concerned with:

a) the rights, freedoms and liberties of the individual,
b) the actions of Governments,
c) the administration of justice, and
d) the reform of laws.'

We also consider that the use of the word 'reasonably' in sub-section 2 may be given to restrictive interpretation. However, it is felt that some element of 'reasonableness' may be necessary for the proper definition of a right of assembly.

3.7 *Picketing*

It is NCCL policy that a statutory right to demonstrate, having priority over other legal rights, must include meetings, processions and pickets.

The Government proposes to apply to pickets the stringent new powers of conditions on static demonstrations (see Chapter 11 below). It concludes that 'where picketing threatens to result in serious public disorder, serious disruption or the coercion of individuals, it is right that it should be subject to the same controls as other forms of static demonstration.'[13] Once the police consider that any of these tests is infringed they will be able to restrict the picketing without reference to location, numbers and duration.

3.8 But no doubt most employers would consider any picketing (particularly effective picketing) to be 'seriously disruptive'. No doubt strike-breakers going to work past a picket would consider themselves subject to 'the coercion of individuals'. If the police accept either view they can act accordingly. The new police power to impose conditions on location, numbers and duration will enable the police to restrict the right of peaceful picketing to the point of utter ineffectiveness. For example, the police will be able to allow just one picket on the front gate of a factory premises for half an hour. Any further picketing would be unlawful and a criminal offence.

3.9 Thus the Government's assurance that 'the right of peaceful picketing will not in any way be infringed'[14] is less than convincing. The Government may say that it does not intend that the power should be used 'to undermine the right of pickets in reasonable numbers to stand by the entrance to a workplace', but their proposals say otherwise.

3.10 Moreover, the history of the law and practice relating to picketing inspires little confidence. The lower courts have a growing tendency to assume, unless the evidence clearly proves otherwise, that the police have exercised their discretion properly in the handling of pickets. Higher courts have expended much energy this century in minimising statutory immunities from civil proceedings in trade disputes.[15] In February 1985, in order to outlaw mass picketing and demonstrations in support of picketing, a judge in South Wales invented a new common law test of intimidation[16], described as unreasonable harassment of those exercising their right to be on the highway.[17] The picketing or presence in its support was unlawful even if completely silent and peaceful.[18]

3.11 NCCL therefore *recommends* that a *right to picket,* ancillary to the right of assembly, should be enacted.

3.12 There is nothing new in trying to modify the rights of pickets through the law. Section 2 of the Trade Disputes Act 1906, sought to redress the hostility of the common law to strikes and pickets. It did not make picketing legal, but provided that it was not necessarily illegal if in a limited form. Modifications have been provided in the Trade Disputes Act 1927, the Industrial Relations Act 1971, the Trade Union and Labour Relations Act 1974, and the Employment Act 1980. The combined limitations imposed by statute and case law now present very modest immunities for

13

pickets from civil suits which might be brought against them for breach of contract or conspiracy or intimidation. At the same time these limitations provide for wide police discretion over pickets on alleged public order grounds.

3.13 The balance can only be redressed by new law. This must provide for:

– the right to attend in contemplation or furtherance of a trade dispute at or near any place or employment for the purpose of obtaining or communicating information or of peacefully persuading others to work or abstain from work

– a defence to any civil or criminal proceedings for a person to be acting peacefully (and reasonably) in accordance with the section.

NCCL appreciates that drafting a right of peaceful picketing is not an easy task and would therefore welcome further discussion on this subject.

3.14 NCCL also takes the view that *the right to picket should extend to consumer picketing.* In *Hubbard v Pitt*[19] the Court of Appeal approved an injunction against small groups of people picketing premises of estate agents. The injunction was granted on the ground that the use of the highway for picketing which was not in contemplation or furtherance of a trade dispute was unlawful, despite the following description of their behaviour: 'There was no obstruction, no violence, no intimidation, no molestation, no noise, no smells, nothing except a group of six or seven people standing about with placards and leaflets outside the plantiffs' premises, all quite orderly and well-behaved.'[20]

However, in an American case[21] the Supreme Court decided that a state trespass law could not be applied to prevent peaceful picketing of a supermarket in a private shopping centre. Also the Royal Commission on Trade Unions and Employers' Associations[22] has recommended that statutory protection be extended to cover consumer picketing.

3.15 *Use of the Highway*

In order to be effective, a positive right of assembly must take priority over other legal rights, notably the right to use the highway as the following paragraphs will explain. As we have already shown (in para 3.2 above) the law gives undue prominence to the right of passage along the highway. In the latest of a long line of judicial decisions restricting the use of the highway for any purpose other than passing to and fro, the Court of Appeal remitted a recent case back to the magistrates with a direction to convict.[23] The defendant, a busker who had been charged with obstructing the highway[24] (a charge often used against demonstrators), had been acquitted by the magistrates, more it would seem for his skill at juggling with lighted fire sticks than for a good defence in law. But the prosecution appealed and the Court of Appeal, having reviewed the previous decisions, (which mostly concerned the use of the highway by mobile snack bars and hot dog stands), came to this far-reaching conclusion:

'In so far as the highway is concerned, members of the public have the right to pass and re-pass along it. That does not, however, mean that one must keep moving all the time. However, if one does stop on a highway then prima facie an obstruction occurs, because by stopping you are on the very piece of the highway that somebody else may wish to pass and re-pass along. Where, however, your stopping is really part and parcel of passing and re-passing along the highway and is ancillary to it (such as a milkman stopping to leave a milk bottle on the doorstep) then this is not an obstruction within the meaning of the subsection with which we are concerned. On the other hand, where stopping on the highway cannot properly be said to be ancillary to or part and parcel of the exercise of one's right to pass and re-pass along that highway, then the obstruction becomes unreasonable and there is an obstruction contrary to the provisions of the subsection.'[25]

Thus every protest of more than minimal numbers, whether static or moving, is prima facie an obstruction, and therefore those taking part will only avoid arrest through the exercise of discretion in their favour on the part of the police.

3.16 Accordingly we *recommend* that the offence of obstruction of the highway should be recast to include the following elements:

– the obstruction of a person's or vehicle's use of the highway must be actual and not merely theoretical
– the obstruction must be significant in time and effect[26]
– the obstruction must be unreasonable in all the circumstances
– the obstruction must be caused intentionally
– the obstruction must be unlawful. It will be lawful if caused in pursuance of paragraph 1 of the right of assembly. (see 3.6 above)

3.17 *Street collections etc.*
The law relating to street collecting[27], leafletting and selling

papers is a confusion of uncertain restrictions. Some police forces still use the laws against begging and peddling under the Vagrancy Act 1824 to remove those who wish to support causes or disseminate views. Local authorities also have a multitude of powers by way of byelaws to restrict what may be done, for example, in certain streets, parks, and public places. Some byelaws give council officials or the police the power to remove persons infringing the requirements of these local laws. In other areas the police restrict this activity by vigorous enforcement of the highway laws. Many of these areas of the law are rarely tested, although the miners' dispute brought prosecutions for collections in aid of striking miners and their families.

NCCL therefore *recommends rationalisation, simplification and codification of the law relating to street collections etc.* as part of the legal framework of the right of assembly and the use of the highway, and with a view to making the law in this area clearer for both police and public.

3.18 In California the Court of Appeal has upheld First Amendment rights ('Congress shall make no law abridging the freedom of speech') for school employees in an industrial dispute to leaflet at the private business offices of two school board members.

'The right to picket peacefully and truthfully is one of organized labour's lawful means of advertising its grievances to the public, and as such is guaranteed by the Constitution . . . Moreover, where, as here, the picketing or leafletting takes place in a public place, it is entitled to greater protection than otherwise might be true.'[28]

In Holland the courts have held that Article 7 of the Constitution which guarantees freedom of expression renders unlawful regulations to prohibit the use of the highway for 'distributing, advertising or publicity material' without prior permission from the local authority.[29]

3.19 However, under English law there is no constitutional background against which to measure the right of collectors and sellers on the street. The principles have been lost in confusing regulations.

In Hammersmith in London, for example, the police have taken the view that selling magazines is lawful but that collecting money is not. The sale of 'The Miner', a broadsheet supporting the miners' strike, was considered to be illegal because in the view of the police it was not a newspaper but a device to get round the collection regulations. On the other hand it would appear (certainly in the London area) that collecting food or collecting money at street meetings may be permitted.

But practice and police interpretation of the law is erratic. During the miners' strike some Police Commanders in London came to working agreements with miners support groups and after the first few weeks there were no arrests or summonses. In other areas there was constant friction and many arrests for obstruction of the highway, obstruction of the police and under Section 5 of the Public Order Act 1936.

In its worst guise, individual officers have threatened arrest where no arrest power exists, have forced 'cautions' upon collectors without explaining that an admission of guilt was a prerequisite, and have generally relied on the confusion of the law and the ignorance of collectors to cause harassment.

Elsewhere some permits for house-to-house collections (under the 1939 Act) were granted in the miners' strike. But some local authorities delayed the grant or refusal of permits for excessive periods. In Dover, where the Council acted contrary to the legal advice of its officers and refused permits, the miners' support group appealed to the Home Secretary. He delayed his decision until two weeks after the strike had ended – then granted permission. The case was referred to the Local Government Ombudsman.

3.20 NCCL takes the view that there should be a presumption in favour of use of the highway and other public places for street collections. leafletting and selling newspapers. Reasons for refusing to allow these activities should be strictly limited under a simplified and codified set of rules.

4. PUBLIC ORDER OFFENCES – INTRODUCTION

4.1 The Government proposes *a major new range of public order offences*. This is one of the key sections of the White Paper. It represents a dramatic increase in police powers of arrest, and in prosecution powers to bring charges. There is no indication that the proposals will either prevent or curb disorder; but they will certainly curtail the rights of protesters by further limiting the scope of lawful public activity.

4.2 Although the Government proposes to abolish the common law public order offences of riot, rout, unlawful assembly and affray (a decision which NCCL welcomes) it proposes to replace them with new statutory offences of riot, violent disorder and affray, with the extension of the existing offence under Section 5 of the Public Order Act 1936 (threatening, abusive, insulting words or behaviour etc.) and with the possible creation of a further statutory offence of disorderly words or conduct.

4.3 NCCL makes *four broad criticisms of the Government's proposals*.

i)   The White Paper fails to review public order offences in conjunction with police preventive powers (para 4.4 below).
ii) The White Paper fails to carry out a comprehensive review of public order offences (para 4.7).
iii) The proposed new offences are unnecessary because of existing offences (para 4.8).
iv) The White Paper fails to recommend codification of public order offences (para 4.9).

4.4 *Preventive powers*
Offences and preventive powers are closely related and must be considered together; the case for more and wider criminal offences cannot be justified without proper reference to the scope of preventive powers. Some preventive powers are necessary for breaking up disorder. Often the use of dispersal tactics will be sufficient without recourse to bringing charges: the potential brawl after public house closing time, the domestic incident spilling over into the street, youthful aggression breaking into a street fight – this kind of incident is often controlled by police officers exercising their preventive powers without having to bring criminal charges.

4.5 *Preventive powers are extensive under the present law*

i)   Most commonly used is the common law power of arrest without charge; it can be exercised where a breach of the peace has been committed, or is reasonably apprehended, or is likely to be renewed.[1] it is commonly used to break up disturbances and cool off offenders. A police officer may use the power to arrest, move on, or detain (if necessary in a police station) and release the person without charge or take the person to the magistrates' court to be bound over to keep the peace or be of good behaviour (but see NCCL's recommendation on bind-overs at para 6.5 below) although this is not a conviction.[2]

ii) Under common law, entry to private premises may be effected (and is therefore not a trespass) by any person in order to save life or limb or to prevent serious damage to property, or by any person who has reasonable grounds for believing that an offence or breach of the peace has been or is likely to be committed there, for example at a public meeting.[3]

iii) The Criminal Law Act 1967 permits any person to use reasonable force in the prevention of crime or in effecting or assisting in the lawful arrest of offenders.[4] (The use of troops in aid of the civil power to disperse rioters would be justified under this Act, the power of soldiers being equated with the power of ordinary citizens. See *Employment of Troops in Aid of the Civil Power, Manual of Military Law.*)

iv) Any person may endeavour of his own authority to suppress a riot or disperse an unlawful assembly.[5] Indeed the public have a duty to help the police prevent or terminate breaches of the peace, and it may be an offence to refuse to do so.[6]

v)   In addition, police officers have wide powers to prevent obstructions of the highway[7] (see para 3.15 above), and (a most useful weapon) when they are themselves obstructed in the execution of their duty an offence is deemed to have been committed[8], although it is only arrestable without warrant if there is a likelihood of a breach of the peace (in practice this aspect of the offence, which comes about because the statute provides no power of arrest, is largely ignored by the courts).

4.6 Although brief reference is made to police powers at common law, the Government does not see fit to carry out a balancing exercise between powers to control and powers to charge. The result is accordingly unbalanced, and weighs heavily in favour of extending the criminal law and bringing more people before the courts. In our proposals (see Chapter 6 below) we argue that a clearly defined minimum preventive power should stand as the cornerstone of any public order policy.

4.7 *Inadequate review of public order offences*

In seeking sweeping new powers the Government's approach ignores the Criminal Law Revision Committee's cardinal warning that there is 'no virtue in introducing unnecessary complications into the criminal law'.[10]

The proposed new offences complicate the law: by retaining difficult concepts such as 'common purpose' in the offence of riot, by continuing the test of hypothetically present persons such as the 'person of reasonable firmness' in the offence of violent disorder, by extending certain offences from public places to private places, and by taking the criminal law for the first time into the realms of conduct which merely causes annoyance or disturbance.

4.8 *Proposed offences unnecessary*

The proposed new offences are unnecessary also because their underlying themes of violence or threats of violence to persons or property are fully covered by the existing criminal law:

i) Violence to persons – Any form of violence to the person, unless justified for example as an accident or self-defence, is an assault. The traditional definition of assault is an act by which a person intentionally or recklessly causes another to apprehend immediate and unlawful violence or an act by which a person intentionally or recklessly inflicts personal violence upon another. The present range of *assault charges*[11] covers:
    – common assault
    – assault occasioning actual bodily harm
    – causing or inflicting grievous bodily harm
    – malicious wounding
    – wounding or causing grievous bodily harm with intent
    – manslaughter
    – murder

ii) Threats to persons – The above definition of assault includes the threat of violence to the person[12] (The Criminal Law Review Committee proposed that threats should be retained within the definition of assault). For clarity it may be better to divide the present definition of assault into two offences: assault involving actual violence (battery) and threat of assault. A threat to kill is an offence under Section 16 of the Offences against the Person Act 1961.

iii) Violence to property – A similar range of offences from simple criminal damage to arson with intent to endanger life is provided by the Criminal Damage Act 1971.

iv) Threats to property – A threat to destroy and damage property is an offence contrary to Section 2, Criminal Damage Act 1971.

v) Attempt – It is an offence contrary to the Criminal Attempts Act 1981 to attempt to commit any of the offences set out above.

vi) Joint enterprise – Under the law of joint enterprise, two or more persons may be charged with any of the above offences as being persons all concerned in committing that offence whether as principals in its commission or by assistance or by encouragement.

vii) Offensive weapons – It is an offence contrary to the Prevention of Crime Act 1953 to have an offensive weapon in a public place.

These are specific offences. In each case the person charged must be proved to have done a specific act before he or she can be convicted. The penalties range from fines to life imprisonment.

4.9 *No codification*

The White Paper fails to see the need for codification of public order powers. The Government prefers to rely on the 'flexibility' of the common law. This is a surprising attitude since the lengthy deliberations and recommendations of the Criminal Law Review Committee into 'Offences against the Person' were adapted for inclusion into a draft Criminal Code which was laid before Parliament by the Law Commission in March 1985.[12] The White Paper's proposals are wholly inconsistent with this approach.

5. PUBLIC ORDER OFFENCES – THE GOVERNMENT'S PROPOSALS

RIOT

5.1 *At common law*

At common law the offence of riot included the elements of at least three persons carrying out a common purpose with force and violence in such a manner as to alarm at least one person of reasonable firmness and courage and with intent to help one another by force if necessary if any person should oppose them in the execution of their purpose.[1] The core of the crime lay in the common purpose (as with unlawful assembly) and in the execution of the common purpose 'in a violent and turbulent manner'.[2] It was considered that the gathering of numbers of people in public places with a common purpose required special powers and special punishment. Severe sentences were necessary, said the Court of Appeal in upholding prison sentences on young undergraduates in the Cambridge Garden House Hotel case.[3] In Nottingham an eighteen-year old man was sentenced to three years' imprisonment for incitement to riot after posting leaflets headed 'Burn Babylon Burn', urging people to have bigger and better riots and to destroy the system.[4]

5.2 *The proposed new offence*

The proposed new offence of riot, which carries a maximum penalty of ten years' imprisonment, is aimed at those using violence in a group of twelve or more who use or threaten such violence with a common purpose. The new limit of twelve people derives from the minimum number which was required to justify the reading of the Riot Act. ('Reading the Riot Act' – the Riot Act 1714 – was repealed as obsolete in 1967. NCCL welcomes the Government's refusal to comply with calls to revive 'reading the Riot Act' by creating an offence of failing to disperse after a lawful warning.[5]

The wording of the new offence follows the Law Commission's proposed statutory definition of riot:

> 'Where twelve or more persons are present together, whether in a public or private place, using or threatening unlawful violence to persons or property, for some common purpose

22

(which may be inferred from their conduct) and their conduct, taken together, is such as would cause a person of reasonable firmness if present at the scene to fear for his personal safety, each of them who uses unlawful violence for the common purpose commits the offence of riot.'

5.3 This definition gives cause for considerable concern. It is wordy, lengthy and difficult to follow. It retains from the common law offence the key element of 'common purpose', which judges, juries and commentators alike have found difficult to understand. The Law Commission Working Paper suggested that the problem over its definition arose from 'a misconception of what actually is required to be proved.'[6] Should there be proof of a prior plan or agreement upon the action to be taken? How should the common purpose be discovered? Can it be properly inferred from conduct, as the White Paper suggests? Should purpose be equated with motive? Does the function of the term 'common purpose' differ between riot and unlawful assembly (see para 5.13 below)? With these questions left mostly unanswered, it is no wonder that Lord Scarman, in advising against the revival of 'reading the Riot Act', was provoked to say that 'We could well find ourselves in a forensic confusion as great as that which prevails now when a jury has the complex task of deciding whether the necessary elements of riot (or unlawful assembly) have been proved.'[7]

5.4 Do we need an offence of riot? The White Paper does not answer this question. It admits that the present charge is 'the least frequently used of the various public order offences'.[8] The justification for a riot offence is given in the Law Commission's report by relying on a passage from the Cambridge Garden House Hotel case:

'(Riot) derives its great gravity from the single fact that the persons concerned were acting in numbers and using these numbers to achieve their purpose . . . the law of this country has always leant heavily against those who, to attain such a purpose, use the threat that lies in the power of numbers.'[9]

This quotation, however, ignores the distinction between offence and penalty. The offence is unnecessary if there are other simpler offences available with adequate maximum penalties to reflect the gravity of its commission in context. The punishment may be increased if the defendant must bear responsibility not only for his or her own conduct but also for a share in the overall conduct of the disturbance (although under the Italian and Cuban

Penal Codes, with certain exceptions, it is a mitigating factor that the offender has acted under the influence of a 'mass suggestion' or a general riot).[10]

As shown in para 4.8 above the range of specific offences is impressive and certainly adequate to cover the use of 'unlawful violence' in the Government's proposed definition.

5.5 Doubts are of course raised that the justification cited is not the true one. There are two other major factors at play. First, riot trials arising out of major disturbances, such as in 1981, are seen by prosecuting authorities as important show trials, a form of public blood-letting after the event. As such there is a real danger that defendants will be selected almost at random to fulfil their public role. Usually they are defendants who have already been charged with specific offences which are then left in abeyance while the riot trial proceeds. Often these cases develop into long drawn out 'political trials' with much discussion of the true 'common purpose'.

5.6 Secondly, there is a widely-held belief that some defendants are charged with riot because there is insufficient evidence to charge them with specific offences of violence to the person or property. The Law Commission Working Party expounded this argument:

> 'It seems to us that where large numbers of rioters are involved there may be overwhelming evidential difficulties in charging the commission of some of the more serious (specific) offences.'

The danger of using what one academic writer called 'a crime of the utmost importance in the law of public order'[12] to circumvent 'evidential difficulties' in proving guilt is self-evident.

5.7 Even the Law Commission's illustration does not support their own case. A mob engaged in a serious disturbance in the streets causes widespread damage to property and injury to persons. The defendant is seen to throw several pieces of paving-stone, but there is no evidence that the result of his acts was to cause personal injury or damage to property, perhaps because many other missiles were being thrown by others at the same time or because, in the confusion of the disturbance, it is impossible for the police to ascertain what has happened. The Law Commission argues that the charge of riot may be appropriate because it may be impossible to prove any other offence except the summary offence under Section 5, Public Order Act, 1936, where the maximum penalty of six months' imprisonment may not reflect the seriousness of the defendant's participation in the riot.

This would appear to be a mistaken view of the law. In the illustration, the defendant is guilty of:

a) Criminal damage contrary to Section 1, Criminal Damage Act, 1971 (maximum penalty ten years' imprisonment). – There is no need to prove that the pieces of paving-stone which he threw actually caused damage. He is party to a joint enterprise with others to cause damage and is therefore jointly responsible with others (the 'mob'), named or unnamed, who as the illustration states caused 'widespread damage to property.' Even if the defendant does not specifically intend to damage property he will nevertheless be guilty of the offence for 'being reckless as to whether any such property would be destroyed or damaged' (Section 1.1).

b) Assault – The defendant is guilty of common assault (maximum penalty twelve months' imprisonment, to run either concurrently with or in addition to the penalty for criminal damage),[14] because he has done an act which intentionally or recklessly causes another person, named or unnamed, to apprehend immediate and unlawful violence (see definition of assault at para 4.8 above). Alternatively, the defendant is guilty of assault if he is a party to a joint enterprise causing 'injury to persons'. The particular offence will depend upon the injuries caused, but at the minimum where some harm is caused he will be guilty of the offence of assault occasioning actual bodily harm contrary to Section 47, Offences Against the Person Act 1861 (maximum penalty five years' imprisonment).

c) Possession of an offensive weapon. It is at least arguable that in the circumstances the defendant is guilty of the offence contrary to Section 1 of the Prevention of Crime Act 1953, of having an offensive weapon, namely a paving stone, with him in a public place (maximum penalty two years' imprisonment). It would have to be argued either that the paving stone was in the circumstances 'adapted for use for causing injury to the person' or that it was 'intended for such use' (Section 1.4) possibly on the basis of intent to intimidate.[15]

5.8 The arguments against the use of riot charges are best illustrated by the Bristol riot trial of 1981.[16] 134 persons were arrested for various public order offences. 16 of them were selected by the Director of Public Prosecutions to face a charge of riot, it being admitted by prosecution lawyers that the selection was to some extent arbitrary. It was of note that none of the 16 had been arrested for riot, but all of them had originally been arrested and charged with specific offences. Of the 16, four were acquitted at the committal proceedings in the magistrates' court. A further three were acquitted on the judge's direction in the Crown Court, five more were acquitted by the jury, who failed to agree on the remaining four defendants. In due course the DPP decided to proceed no further against the last four. The trial did not take place until ten months after the riot. It cost about £500,000, roughly the same cost as the riot damage. The DPP commented that it might have been a mistake to bring riot charges at all. But from start to finish the defendants were subject to an extremely serious charge and, if convicted, would no doubt have received long terms of imprisonment.

5.9 The proposed maximum penalty of ten years' imprisonment is, in any event, too long. No defendant should be sentenced to a lengthy term of imprisonment without specific proof of the commission of serious violence in which case a specific charge should be laid to prove it.

5.10 More recently the collapse of a number of riot cases arising out of the miners' strike has cast serious doubts upon the future of the offence of riot. 'The Collapse of Unstout Cases', as *The Guardian* expressed it, has been spectacular.

A short three-week history illustrates the collapse. The Sheffield Crown Court was the principal venue for these remarkable events. On 15 July 1985, thirteen pickets were acquitted by a jury of riot and unlawful assembly arising out of incidents outside the National Coal Board headquarters in Doncaster. The case took fourteen months to reach the stage of a trial, lasted eight weeks and cost an estimated £250,000. On 17 July 1985 the prosecution dropped charges of riot at the Orgreave Coke Works on the forty-eighth day of a trial costing at least £300,000. On 19 July 1985 the prosecution announced their intention to proceed with riot and unlawful assembly charges against miners at their own colliery at Rossington in South Yorkshire. But on 22 July 1985 the case was not proceeded with after the defendants agreed to be bound over for one year in the sum of £100. On 25 July 1985, charges of unlawful assembly were dropped against five men involved in disturbances at Rossington colliery when they admitted specific offences, including arson, burglary, theft and handling. On 5 August 1985, the prosecution offered no evidence (and no bind-over) against seventy-nine miners charged with riot or unlawful assembly at Orgreave.

By October 1985, although some cases were still pending, 440 men had been charged with riot or unlawful assembly or both in Nottinghamshire and South Yorkshire, and no jury had returned a verdict of guilty.

5.11 These cases have, however, proved something more than the difficulties faced by prosecutors and the danger faced by defendants. In the second Rossington case, pleas of guilty to specific criminal activity were clearly more suitable than catch-all offences. In the Doncaster case the disturbance was neither a riot in law nor in common parlance, but political overtures (notably from the then Home Secretary, Mr Leon Brittan, in a number of speeches) had increased the stakes. In all the cases the delay to trial was excessive. And, most sinister of all, in the Orgreave case police officers admitted that parts of their witness statements had been dictated by a South Yorkshire detective, one officer was accused by a Home Office forensic scientist of forging a colleague's signature and generally the evidence presented completely failed to match the sweeping claims made by prosecuting counsel at the opening of the case. As the local newspaper in Sheffield, the *Morning Telegraph*, put it:

> 'The prosecution case often seemed flimsy and progressed – if it progressed – only at the expense of grave embarrassment to the police, where methods of preparing the case often seemed careless and sometimes seemed improper.'

One defence barrister went further and called it 'the worst example of a mass frame-up in this country this century.'

5.12 *Rout*

NCCL welcomes the abolition of the obsolete offence of rout, which falls uncertainly somewhere between riot and unlawful assembly.

5.13 *Unlawful Assembly/Violent Disorder*

NCCL welcomes the abolition of the common law offence of unlawful assembly. The true definition of an unlawful assembly has remained elusive, a clear example of the dangers of leaving the criminal law to the shifting sands of the common law, to interpretation by judges as opposed to statutory definition by Parliament. Academics, text book writers and senior appeal court judges[19] have all differed in construing this offence. In essence, an unlawful assembly occurs when three or more persons assemble together, with a common purpose to commit a crime by violence. Sometimes it is called an embryonic or incipient riot, in that the elements of riot are present except that the violent common purpose has not yet been carried out.

5.14 In recent times unlawful assembly has been used with mixed success against, for example, football hooligans, rival gangs of Hell's Angels, rampaging students and flying pickets. It has often been used by prosecutors in cases where nothing else seems to be appropriate. In 1973 NCCL defended five building workers who were charged together with an ATV television crew with unlawful assembly and conspiracy to trespass.[20] The building workers, followed and filmed by the ATV crew, had entered an employment bureau at Birmingham to protest against the bureau's employment of 'lump' labour contrary to an agreement between unions and employers. Once inside the bureau, the protesters barricaded themselves in and showed employment cards to the television camera. When the police arrived there was no violence, nor any arrests. But subsequently the defendants were summonsed. Unknown to the prosecution, the defendants had a cast-iron defence to conspiracy to trespass under an Act of 1875. The jury acquitted them on the remaining charge of unlawful assembly.[21]

5.15 In place of unlawful assembly the Government proposes *a new offence of violent disorder*, which will carry a maximum penalty of five years' imprisonment. It is intended for use as 'the normal charge for serious outbreaks of public disorder',[22] and will catch those in a group of three or more using or threatening unlawful violence to persons or property. The full proposed offence is as follows:

> 'Where three or more persons are present together using or threatening unlawful violence to persons or property, whether in a public or private place, and their conduct, taken together, is such that it would cause a person of reasonable firmness if present at the scene to fear for his personal safety, each of those persons who uses or threatens unlawful violence commits the offence of violent disorder.'

5.16 If the recent disasters encountered by riot cases do not render the offence of riot obsolete, the creation of the offence of violent disorder will almost certainly do so. There will be few, if any, occasions when prosecutors will seek a greater penalty than five years' imprisonment. Moreover, this offence is the offence of riot with a minimum of three persons, not twelve, and no requirement to prove a 'common purpose'.

5.17 But the weaknesses remain. The offence is too wide, too uncertain. The hypothetical 'person of reasonable firmness' need not be present, and the use of the words 'or threatens', added contrary to the wishes of the Law Commission, makes the offence wider in scope than the lesser offence of threatening behaviour, contrary to Section 5 of the Public Order Act 1936. Any youth, for example, in a group of three or more, who walks along the road after public house closing time and shouts any kind of idle and unintended threat at any person (or about any absent person) in an otherwise empty street will fall foul of this offence.

Further, this offence, which lacks simplicity and clarity, is amply covered by specific offences of violence or threats of violence to persons or property (set out at para 4.8 above). It is therefore yet another unnecessary complication to the criminal law.

5.18 *Affray*

The old common law offence of affray, which means 'fighting to the public terror', was considered for many years to be obsolete, until its modern revival in 1957.[23] Now it is charged against some 1,000 people a year, a statistic which encourages the White Paper[24] to claim that it has 'a useful part to play in the calendar of public order offences'.

5.19 In practice affray is an overworked charge which substantially increases the length and cost of criminal trials. It is almost always an unnecessary charge because the defendants have been charged with specific assaults or with specific acts of criminal damage or with possessing offensive weapons, such as the carrying of knives or the smashing of bottles in the heat of the moment. Fighting, it should be remembered, even by consent, is an assault.[25] At a case in Chelmsford in July 1985, for example, all six defendants who were later charged with an affray at a holiday camp had either been originally charged with specific criminal activity or were seen or had admitted committing specific criminal activity which was later used to prove the offence of affray. The use of affray charges added nothing to the weight of the case, nor to the length of sentences imposed on conviction.

5.20 Otherwise affray is often used where proof of specific activity is absent or difficult, a justification specifically endorsed by appellate judges in 1966.[26] But the taking of evidential short cuts may lead to the wrongful conviction of those who are present but not participating in any criminal activity. The prosecution should either prove that the defendant was engaged in specific criminal activity or that he was jointly responsible under the properly-invoked law of joint enterprise for the criminal acts of others. Otherwise there should be no charge, no prosecution. This approach does not ignore the realities of street fighting.[27] It protects those possibly innocent persons, who are with others in the street, from the risk of conviction on inadequate evidence, usually of the 'you were there, so you must have been involved' variety.

5.21 The proposed new offence of affray does nothing to allay these fears. It provides:

'Where two or more persons use or threaten unlawful violence against each other, or one or more persons use or threaten unlawful violence against another, whether in a public or private place, and the conduct of those using or threatening unlawful violence is such as would cause a person of reasonable firmness if present at the scene to fear for his personal safety, each of them commits the offence of affray.'

5.22 *Section 5, Public Order Act 1936, Amended*
The offence of threatening, abusive or insulting words or behaviour with intent to provoke a breach of the peace or whereby a breach of the peace is likely to be occasioned, contrary to Section 5, Public Order Act 1936, can only be tried in the magistrates' courts. The maximum penalty on convicition is six months' imprisonment or a fine of £2,000 or both. Despite its frequent use and its place at the bottom of the list of public order offences, this is often treated as a serious charge. Those convicted of this offence arising out of football matches, often on uncertain evidence, can expect to go to prison.

5.23 However, Section 5 has been so widely construed by the courts and is so often used by police and prosecutors that it has come to mean all things to all people, a catch-all charge for any possible minor infringement of public order law. In NCCL's submissions on the 1936 Public Order Bill the precursor to Section 5 was criticized:

'The Council's experience is that a strained interpretation is frequently put on this offence by magistrates. For example, an unemployed man was fined some years ago for using the words: "Give us bread". The Council considers, therefore, that any extension of this vague and elastic offence is dangerous and they would, indeed, welcome its total repeal.'

5.24 Subsequent experience has shown that as a minimum standard for criminal activity in a public order context Section 5 continues to be too wide and too uncertain. The charge has been laid against some 4,000 miners in the miners' strike, sometimes only for shouting 'Scab'. As one academic lawyer has described it, Section 5 is used 'from time to time as a form of dragnet provision against those whose behaviour is considered by the police and the courts to be worthy of punishment.'[28] It has been used against a heckler who complained to Willy Brandt about 'krauts', against a protestor who called out 'Remember Biafra' during the ceremony of two minutes silence at the Cenotaph in Whitehall on Remembrance Day, and in consecutive years against revellers in the Trafalgar Square fountains, one who took off his clothes in the second tier and one who threw a bucket of water over the crowd.

NCCL still supports the repeal of the existing Section 5 offence, as we advocated in 1935.

5.25 However, the Government proposes to amend and extend Section 5 with two major changes.

i)   Private Places

The Government proposes to extend the scope of Section 5 from public places – at present broadly defined as any place to which the public have access whether on payment or otherwise – to private places (with the exception of private dwelling houses). This extension makes for an unnecessary increase of police involvement in the private domain. The proposal would extend the offence to factories, offices, private meetings, shareholders' meetings and private clubs. The police would have powers to arrest an employee for insulting behaviour to an employer, shareholders for threatening words at company meetings, and members of private clubs for letting off steam at one another. These are all situations which are dealt with by civil proceedings or disciplinary means or rules which are part of the self-regulation of workplaces and private associations. Police involvement would not only be unnecessary but, in most cases, unwelcome and may of itself increase the conflict.

The apparent justification for this proposal is that during the miners' strike some Section 5 summonses against striking miners were dismissed because the threatening words were uttered from private land towards those who were on the highway.[29] These cases have not been tested on appeal (to the writer's knowledge), and the justification appears to be a flimsy excuse in any event.

ii)   'Likely to cause another person to fear unlawful violence'

The extended reformulation of Section 5 – from words or behaviour 'whereby a breach of the peace is likely to be occasioned' to words or behaviour 'likely to cause another person to fear unlawful violence or to provoke the use of unlawful violence by another' – is intended to overturn two sensible decisions of the High Court (*Marsh v. Arscott*[30] and *Parkin v. Norman*[31]). These cases decided that where there was no likelihood of a breach of the peace, because, for example, the only persons present were police officers or an elderly lady passing by on the other side of the road who were not expected to retaliate, no offence was committed.

This is an extremely important point of public order law. The

31

balance must be set between preventive powers and criminal offences; the line must be drawn between criminal conduct and other behaviour falling short of conduct which needs to be penalised. On this aspect the Government ignores the question of balance, yet draws the line further and further towards conduct which has hitherto remained unstigmatized with the criminal law – both with the reformulated Section 5 offence and with the new offence of disorderly conduct (see para 5.27 below). The new wording requires no proof of a breach of the peace, no proof of a likelihood of a breach of the peace, not even proof that unlawful violence was actually feared. Nor does the White Paper accept the Law Commission's proposal that the fear should be of *immediate* violence.

5.26 The Government would do well to remember the words of Lord Justice Lawton in the case of *Ambrose*[32] in which the Court of Appeal quashed a Section 5 conviction for the use of rude or offensive words:

> 'It is important that Section 5 of the Public Order Act should not be misused. It is clear from the long title to that Act why it was passed and the Court notices with regret that in recent years there has been a tendency to use the provisions of Section 5 for the purposes which were not within the intentions of Parliament.'

5.27 *Disorderly Conduct*

Somewhat tentatively the White Paper puts forward for consideration a new offence at the bottom end of the public order scale, of disorderly conduct. The main elements of the new offences are;

a) 'threatening, abusive, insulting or disorderly words or behaviour in or within view of a public place,
b) behaviour which causes substantial alarm, harassment or distress.'

It is clear that this offence would be much wider than a Section 5 offence (even if amended as the White Paper proposes). This is a disturbing proposal. It moves far beyond the scope of violence or threats of violence to persons or property, and, in its generality, embraces a whole range of activity which may be anti-social, which may cause a degree of annoyance or disturbance, but which should not, in the view of NCCL, be classified as criminal behaviour.

5.28 The White Paper concedes that it is not easy to define an offence which is sufficiently general to catch the variety of conduct aimed at. It concedes that there would be justifiable objections to a wide extension of the criminal law. It concedes that not every degree of annoyance or disturbance will suffice.[33]

5.29 But the examples quoted of conduct which would fall under the terms of the new offence include hooligans on housing estates peering in at windows and knocking over dustbins, groups of youths pestering people in queues or turning out the lights in a dance hall, and rowdy behaviour late at night. To this list must be added any group of people making a noise in public: loud talking on the way home from a meeting, teenagers leaving the local disco, shutting car doors after a party, children playing on an estate.

5.30 NCCL views this proposal with grave concern:

1) NCCL is against any criminal offence which, in attempting to deal with disturbance and inconvenience, deals merely with a wide variety of anti-social behaviour and which inevitability will lack precise definition. As the National Association of Probation Officers has said:

> 'NAPO acknowledges that the apparent increase in disorderly behaviour causes all responsible people concern. However, it is our belief that the introduction of a new offence of disorderly behaviour will place many of our young clients, prone to boisterous and extrovert behaviour, at risk of arrest by over-reactive policing.'

2) NCCL believes that the application of this offence may exacerbate the poor relations between police and public, particularly between the police and young people and racial minorities – where the use of arrest powers for this offence (given to the police under the Police and Criminal Evidence Act 1984) may itself lead to public disorder.

3) NCCL believes that the criterion for public order controls should be a minimum test of actual violence or threats of violence to persons or property (see para 6.1 below). The public disorder test should be the sole basis for police action. Much of the activity which the Government envisages will be caught by the offence of disorderly conduct, and will therefore fall outside the scope of this test.

4) It is not enough to say, as the organisation Justice has suggested, that the Home Office should issue 'careful guidelines as to how this offence is to be policed if it is enacted.' Once enacted, police officers will be entitled to exercise their own discretion within their understanding of the law. The offence is

wrong in principle. It cannot be improved by the exercise of police discretion.

5) Enforcing the offence would involve the considerable use of police resources, which would be better employed elsewhere. Many of the complaints from housing estates result from the bad design of the estates, from poor management of them and from the placement of elderly people in vulnerably-sited accommodation – these are the conclusions of the Bramshill Police Training College's report 'A Co-ordinated Approach' and of proposals for a fresh approach to crime on estates by the National Association for the Care and Re-settlement of Offenders.

5.31 *Alternative Verdicts*

The Government also proposed that in the new statutory scale of offences all the lesser offences should be available as alternative verdicts to any of the more serious charges. This will apply to both Crown Court and Magistrates' Court trials.

5.32 NCCL opposes this proposal. It would mean that where a defendant faces a charge of riot he or she could be convicted of any public order offence (triable on indictment) without the requirement for that offence being specified or read out in court. Similarly, in the magistrates' court a defendant charged with violent disorder could be convicted of a Section 5 offence or of disorderly conduct. It means in practice that the defendant is defending not only the elements in the offence charged but all the other elements in the lesser offences as well.

5.33 This proposals is a substantial departure from the present law. At present a verdict for a lesser offence can only be taken in limited circumstances:

a) if it is particularly charged, in circumstances in which the defendant knows, not only the offence charged but the particular facts which the prosecution will rely on; or

b) under the 'blue pencil test', which is strictly limited, so that for example a defendant charged with wounding with intent can also be convicted of wounding (the words 'with intent' having been deleted by 'the blue pencil' test) but not of any other offence except where expressly charged.

5.34 The proposed approach to alternative verdicts has a number of serious defects. It lays a defendant open to conviction for an offence for which he or she has not been charged and of which the particulars have not been supplied. More particularly in the magistrates' court, defendants are frequently unrepresented because legal aid is invariably not made available for public order offences, except after conviction when a prison sentence is in view.

Unrepresented defendants may address their case, their evidence and their arguments to the ingredients of the offence charged, only to find that the court has another offence altogether in mind. This proposal should not be accepted.

6. PUBLIC ORDER OFFENCES – THE ALTERNATIVE APPROACH

NCCL'S PROPOSALS

6.1 *The public disorder test*

As we have already indicated (in para 5.30 above) NCCL believes that the sole criterion for public order controls should be a minimum test of actual violence or immediate threat of violence to persons or property. The threat of violence must be immediate in the sense that it must be proximate in time and place.

This test is taken from the definition of breach of the peace in the Court of Appeal decision in *Howell:*[1].

> 'The statement in Halsbury ("a breach of the peace arises where there is an actual assault, or where public alarm and excitement are caused by a person's wrongful act. . .") is in parts, we think, inaccurate because of its failure to relate all the kinds of behaviour there mentioned to violence. Furthermore, we think, the word "disturbance" when used in isolation cannot constitute a breach of the peace. We are emboldened to say that there is a breach of the peace whenever harm is actually done or is likely to be done to a person or in his presence to his property or a person is in fear of being so harmed through an assault, (an affray, a riot, unlawful assembly or other disturbance). It is for this breach of the peace when done in his presence or the reasonable apprehension of it taking place that a constable, or anyone else, may arrest an offender without warrant.'

Other attempts at defining a breach of the peace (for example by Lord Denning in the *Luxulyan* case[2]) are too wide and fail to incorporate essential elements into an effective public disorder test. This test, akin to the American 'clear and present danger' test, would, for example, outlaw police road blocks to control the movement of persons and traffic on the ground that a breach of the peace might possibly take place at some distant place in the future (which was the justification for stopping miners at the Dartford Tunnel).[3]

6.2 *Police preventive powers*

As we have indicated in our broad criticisms of the Government's proposals on public order offences (see para 4.3 above) the Government has failed to consider sufficiently these important police powers to disperse people where public disorder takes place and to arrest and if necessary detain without charge. We have set out the extensive existing preventive powers at para 4.5 above. NCCL *recommends* that these various preventive powers should be clarified, modified and codified.

6.3 NCCL accordingly recommends that the sole basis for police preventive powers should be the public disorder test of violence or immediate threat of violence to persons or property.

6.4 NCCL further *recommends* that the exercise of the preventive arrest power for public disorder should follow the principles of *Howell:*

> 'We hold that there is power of arrest for breach of the peace where: (1) a breach of the peace is committed in the presence of the person making the arrest or (2) the arrester reasonably believes that such a breach will be committed in the immediate future by the person arrested although he has not yet committed any breach or (3) where a breach has been committed and it is reasonably believed that a renewal of it is threatened.'[4]

6.5 NCCL further *recommends* that the preventive arrest power for public disorder should be limited to dispersal or detention (but only where necessary, for example, for preventing two sides from returning to fight; for legitimate cooling off – any unreasonable detention will be actionable in the civil courts as false imprisonment). NCCL *recommends* that the power should not extend to taking the person before a court to be bound over, and that the existing power to do so should be abolished. The person should only be taken before a court where it has been necessary to charge the person with a criminal offence.

6.6 The power of criminal courts to *bind over* persons (including witnesses) who have not been charged with a criminal offence has existed at least since the Justices of the Peace Act 1361, which gave justices of the peace the power 'to take of all them that be (not) of good fame, where they shall be found, sufficient surety and mainprise of their good behaviour towards the King and his people. . . to the intent that the peace be (not) blemished'. Modern statutes have also provided that any person may be bound over to keep the peace and/or be of good behaviour (for the present power see Sections 115 and 116, Magistrates' Courts Act 1980). The proceedings are civil, not criminal, and it is not essential to the exercise of this jurisdiction that the conduct of the defendant should have caused any individual person to go in bodily fear.

6.7 *Public order offences*

NCCL *recommends* that the common law offences of riot, rout, unlawful assembly and affray should be abolished (as the White Paper proposes) and further *recommends* that they should not be replaced by the proposed statutory offences of riot, violent disorder, and affray. NCCL further *recommends* that the offence, contrary to Section 5 of the Public Order Act 1936, should not be amended as proposed but abolished (as we recommended in 1935) and that the proposed offence of disorderly conduct should not be enacted.

For the detailed reasons that we have set out in Chapters 4 and 5 above, NCCL believes –

a) that any offence of public disorder should relate to the preventive police power and should be based on the public disorder test of violence or immediate threat of violence to persons or property; and

b) that the existing laws of assault, criminal damage and offensive weapons (as set out in para 4.8 above) are wholly adequate for the conviction and punishment of offenders within the scope of this test.

6.8 In considering preventive powers and minimum public disorder offences, NCCL gave consideration to replacing the Section 5 offence (see para 5.22 above) with a new statutory offence of public disorder. This offence would have been based on the definition of breach of the peace in *Howell* and would have read as follows:

'Any person who in any public place or any public meeting –
a) does an act which either actually harms a person, or in his presence his property, or
b) threatens to do an act which puts someone in immediate fear of such harm being done,
with intent to cause harm or to threaten that harm should be caused, shall be guilty of an offence.'

The offence would have contained a power of arrest and would have been triable either way, that is with the right to elect trial by jury[6], with a maximum penalty of two years' imprisonment and a fine[7], with legal aid available in all cases, subject to means. It would not have been committed where there was no real likelihood of immediate public disorder.[8]

However, despite being consistent with our proposal on preventive powers and our public disorder test, we concluded that the activity included in the offence is already covered by existing assault and criminal damage charges (see para 4.8 above) and that this offence is therefore unnecessary.

6.9 We further *recommend* that the offence of obstructing a police officer in the execution of his duty[9] should be restricted (as it is in Scotland) to *physical* obstruction. This was the law from 1839, when the first legislation appeared, until the decision in *Duncan v. Jones* in 1936.[10] Until that time, obstruction of the police was considered to involve physical obstruction and was cognate of assault on constables.[11] In *Duncan v. Jones*, a case defended by NCCL, the Divisional Court held that Mrs Duncan, of the National Unemployed Workers' Movement, had been lawfully arrested by a police officer for trying to hold a meeting outside an unemployed training centre (a meeting at which NCCL's first general secretary, Ronald Kidd, was billed to speak). The officer had 'reasonably' feared a breach of the peace because a meeting in the same place a year before had been followed by disturbances inside the training centre. He was therefore entitled to take steps to prevent a breach of the peace.

The decision has been roundly criticised. Professor Brownlie, a leading authority on public order law, has pointed out that:

> 'The decision gives a legislative aspect to the preventative powers themselves and buttresses a discretionary power with criminal sanction.'[12]

Since the decision the courts have upheld extensive police powers to regulate activities, for example, where police officers limited pickets in a trade dispute to two in number at each entrance to a factory.[13] According to our proposal, failing to obey a police order will not *per se* constitute this offence of obstructing a police officer. This may have the necessary controlling effect upon police behaviour. Since the decision in *Duncan v. Jones*, the police have come to believe that they are entitled to give directions to any individual or group of people on the streets in any circumstances, whether the power exists or not. Failure to comply with directions has resulted in numerous unnecessary and misconceived prosecutions for obstructing a police officer in the execution of his duty.

6.10 We *recommend* that the offence of obstruction of the highway should be amended (see para 3.16 above).

6.11 We *recommend* that the powers relating to the carrying of offensive weapons[14] should be amalgamated to conform with Section 1, Prevention of Crime Act 1953 (see para 4.8 above).

6.12 There is no need for a new 'reading the Riot Act' power, namely failing to disperse after a lawful warning. The White Paper pts Lord Scarman's conclusion[15] that none is required.

6.13 The White Paper proposes that the offence of intimidation including watching and besetting[16] should be retained, should carry a specific power of arrest and should have an increased maximum penalty of six months imprisonment or £2,000 fine. We *recommend* that the offence be abolished. It is archaic in its wording and, in view of our proposals above, unnecessary. The wording of this statute is so vague that it has been applied to sit-ins in factories[17] as well as to situations where a charge of assault or threatening criminal damage would have been more suitable. Otherwise it has been used in circumstances which fall short of our public disorder test and therefore in which the use of civil proceedings to restrain or prevent behaviour would have been more appropriate.

7. INCITEMENT TO RACIAL HATRED

7.1 The Government proposes to re-cast the offence of incitement to racial hatred contained in Section 5A of the Public Order Act 1936 to penalise conduct intended to stir up racial hatred as well as that likely to do so, to remove the exemption for material published or distributed within an association, but not to extend the offence to broadcasting. A new offence of possessing racially inflammatory material with a view to distribution or publication is proposed.

7.2 *Conduct intended to stir up racial hatred*
NCCL welcomes the moves to strengthen the law against stirring up racial hatred. It is right to penalise conduct which is *intended* to stir up racial hatred even though it may not be possible to prove that it is likely to do so. This arises where those confronted with the conduct either agree with it or are so implacably opposed to it that there is no chance of their being influenced by it. But for the present inadequacy of the law, two of the best known failed prosecutions would probably have been successful. The first case concerned the delivery of inflammatory material, a pamphlet entitled 'Blacks not wanted here', to Sidney Bidwell MP. The Court of Appeal decided that distribution of a pamphlet to the home of a Member of Parliament was not publication to the public at large. The other case was the prosecution of John Kingsley Read, leader of the British Movement, who addressed his supporters, after an Asian youth was killed in Southall, with the words 'One down, a million to go.'

7.3 *Publication within an association*
NCCL also welcomes the removal of the exemption for publication or distribution to members of an association. There is a real need to bring within the law the underground distribution of obnoxious material to members of amorphous organisations like the National Front, where there is nothing approaching a private or personal relationship between the members. There is an argument, put forward for example by *Justice,* that the right to freedom of expression, guaranteed by Article 10 of the European Convention on Human Rights, requires that where unpopular associations are permitted a legal existence, they should enjoy freedom to express their views within their own groups. But even in the case of genuinely private or selective organisations there is a

41

justification for applying the law, because by definition racial incitement has an impact on persons outside the organisation.

7.4 *The power of arrest*

Section 5A is at present not an arrestable offence. By contrast Section 5 of the Public Order Act 1936 (threatening, abusive, insulting words and behaviour etc.) carries the power of arrest. It is a restraint on police action which should be remedied. We therefore *recommend* that Section 5A should become an arrestable offence.

7.5 *The Attorney General's consent*

We further *recommend* that the Attorney General's consent to prosecution should be dispensed with[2]. It is a serious weakness in the White Paper that this proposal is not made. The present Attorney General is reluctant to authorise prosecutions because he believes, questionably, that an unsuccessful prosecution does more harm than good to racial equality. Furthermore the consent requirement discourages the police from bringing charges in many cases where they would otherwise do so. There have been many instances where National Front and other fascist activists have carried inflammatory banners or made inflammatory speeches at demonstrations or marches and the police have taken no action. Between 1965 and 1973, for example, only seven prosecutions (against fifteen people) were authorised by the Attorney General.

7.6 *Broadcasting*

The White Paper rejects the idea that Section 5A should be extended to broadcast material. In putting forward this proposal to the Home Affairs Committee, NCCL sympathised with the views expressed by the Commission for Racial Equality who had pointed out that an *Open Door* broadcast expressing racist sentiments had 'caused deep and widespread concern not only amongst the ethnic minority communities but amongst wide sections of the population at large.' The Commission argued, with some force, that it is inconsistent for the dissemination of racial disaffection to be an offence when the audience or readers are numbered merely in tens or hundreds, but for it not to be an offence when, through broadcasting, it reaches an audience of tens or hundreds of thousands[3].

The Government's reasoning, apparently based on the view that the offence could not be confined to the person uttering the words, is illogical. Cable operators are made liable under the Cable and Broadcasting Act 1984, save that they may escape liability if they show that it was not reasonably practicable to remove the offending words before the programme.

We therefore *recommend* that Section 5A should extend to

broadcast material. The individual uttering the offensive words should always be liable and the broadcasting authority and programme producer in the case of any scripted programme.

7.7 *Possessing racially inflammatory material*

NCCL welcomes the proposed new offence of possessing racially inflammatory material with a view to distribution or publication and accepts that it would have no effect without an associated power of search, seizure and forfeiture. The precise wording of a draft offence would, however, need to be looked at with care in order to protect a *bona fide* possessor of offensive material, for example a person handed literature in the street or an organisation collecting material in order to expose its harmful nature.

8. MARCHES AND PROCESSIONS – ADVANCE NOTICE

8.1 The White Paper proposes a new national requirement, with a related offence of non-compliance, for organisers to give advance notice of a march or procession seven days before the event, or as soon as reasonably practicable thereafter, with an exception for processions of a religious, educational or ceremonial character customarily held.

8.2 NCCL has for many years opposed any requirement to give advance notice of demonstrations. NCCL views the proposals as a serious infringement on the right of protest. NCCL therefore *recommends* that there should be no advance notice requirement at either national or local level. NCCL believes that marches and processions are best policed by consent, with the minimum of restriction. We therefore support the widespread practice of voluntary co-operation with the police.

8.3 The spontaneous demonstration is a common phenomenon of protest. Sudden events or political decisions lead people to give expression to their views in public. Often this is the only way their voices can be heard. It may be a Town Hall decision to close play facilities, or it may be the imposition of the death penalty by a foreign power which affects the interests of people in this country. Public reaction is more effective if instant and spontaneous. But the Government's proposals for advance notice within seven days may make the protest illegal and the organisers liable to prosecution.

8.4 The Government argues that the use of the words 'within seven days or as soon as reasonably practicable thereafter' provides the organiser of a spontaneous demonstration with a defence to a criminal charge. But the fact is that the organiser will still be *at risk of prosecution* at the discretion of the police. Many potential organisers will be forced to think long and hard before embarking on a peaceful protest which could lead to their prosecution and a criminal conviction, however small the penalty may be. Others will resent the interference by the police; to them it will seem like a system of licensing public protest. In November 1979, Penny Lloyd, a thirteen-year-old schoolgirl, complained to NCCL that she had been threatened with prosecution under a local byelaw for organising a protest march to a building firm over lack of promised play facilities and for failing to tell the police.

8.5 Other organisers will see the possible breach of the law as a challenge to be met by defiance. The Cameron Commission inquiring into the Derry disorders of 1968 concluded that the involvement of the law in banning part of the civil rights march played a significant part in the violence that ensued. And, as Lord Scarman has pointed out, a £400 fine will pose no real threat to those set upon a course of disorder.

8.6 But the requirement is not only wrong in principle; it is also unnecessary. While many local authorities have rejected the need for the requirement, others who possess it (usually for a period of considerably less than seven days) have not used it to enforce the law. We know of no report of any prosecutions. It is unlikely that there has been no breach of the law. It is more likely that police and prosecuting authorities have not felt the need to use the penalties provided. There is considerable irony in the logic of the White Paper's argument for rejecting a notice provision for static assemblies (see generally Chapter 11 below):

'Discussion of an advance notice requirement has made it clear that it would produce much unnecessary work for the police to little purpose . . . An advance notice requirement would therefore inundate the police with notifications of perfectly peaceful meetings. The administrative burden would far outweigh the information gained[1].

It should also be noted that in the Red Lion Square report, Lord Scarman said that the police had failed to make proper use of the notice they had been given[2].

8.7 The White Paper seeks support for its case from Lord Scarman in the Brixton disorders report[3]. But it fails to record 1) what Merlyn Rees, then Home Secretary, decided in 1978 after a review of notice requirements – that a national provision was unnecessary[4]. 2) It also fails to take account of Lord Scarman's earlier view[5] on advance notice:

'I do not think the need for it has been established: and it does present really insuperable difficulty for the urgently called demonstration. Certainly the lack of any such requirement played no part in the causation of these disorders: for the police had all the notice they needed.

'It cannot be said too often that our law assumes that people will be tolerant, self-disciplined, and willing to co-operate with the police. The assumption is still sound: that is why the police go unarmed, and also why, with no legal requirement of notice, the police are in fact notified in at least 80% of cases. There are some who – law or no law – would never give notice: but they are on the fringe of our society and should not, I suggest, force upon the law a largely unnecessary requirement, which can at times be an embarrassment to law-abiding citizens. In the few instances where no notification is given, the police have so far experienced no difficulty in finding out that a demonstration is planned. An effective demonstration needs a degree of advance publicity: the police, therefore, are seldom ignorant of what is planned. I do not, therefore, recommend this change in the law.'

The White Paper also fails to explain or justify Lord Scarman's change of heart between the two reports. All that Lord Scarman says is that subsequent events have shown the need for the requirement.

8.8 The White Paper proposes a seven-day period, which is notably longer than the seventy-two hours proposed by the Home Affairs Committee. The White Paper takes Scotland as a precedent for the seven-day period, but fails to point out the significant difference in Scotland, namely that notice is given not to the police but to regional councils. It is also of note that many of the local authorities who have enacted local notice provisions have been content with periods considerably shorter than seven days (usually 24 or 36 hours).

8.9 The proposal for advance notice of processions would cause difficulties in the following types of situations:

a) Where a group campaigning for the release of political prisoners abroad discovers that in two days time an important prisoner is to be executed by a foreign government. Public feeling may run so high on this issue that the members of the organisation decide to organise an immediate march to the relevant embassy. In the first instance they will have to rely on police discretion that it was not in fact practicable to have given notice earlier. A refusal by the police to waive the criterion of practicability and a decision to prosecute would inevitability be seen as a political decision.

b) A local factory is emitting dangerous or unpleasant fumes, or a group of parents wish to press for an immediate street crossing the day after a fatal accident caused by the lack of such a crossing. In both circumstances, although it may be impractible to wait for seven days, it will be important to those demonstrating to harness public opinion straightaway and have a march, for example, to make the council realise the necessity of doing something about the immediate danger at once.

c) The local trades council has known for three months that there are likely to be redundancies declared by the local authority. It is not until five days before the important council meeting that the local officials of a number of trade unions finally come to an agreement to hold a march. In practical terms there is no reason why at any of their meetings during the past three months they could not have made the decision to have the march – the delay was a political one.

By carrying on with their protest in these circumstances the organisers would risk prosecution for failing to give advance notice. This risk of prosecution will, in NCCL's view, seriously inhibit the traditional right to demonstrate. As Christian CND have put it:

'In our campaign it is often necessary to call acts of witness or protest at short notice. A week later may be too late to make an effective statement about an issue such as the movement of a Cruise convoy, or a new development in the arms race. We cannot see how advance notice will prevent public disorder; public disorder does occur on marches that the police have prior notice of. What the seven-day notice rule will do is to inhibit public protest, and will amount to the licensing by police of particular demonstrations.'[6]

9 MARCHES AND PROCESSIONS – BANS

9.1 The Government proposes a limited number of important changes to the power to ban processions provided by Section 3 of the Public Order Act 1936. The apprehension of serious public disorder will remain the sole ground for prohibiting processions. There shall be no change to the existing procedure for making banning orders, involving Chief Constables, local authorities and the Home Secretary. A new power to ban a single march or procession is proposed, in addition to the existing provision for blanket or class bans. A new offence of knowingly participating in a prohibited procession is proposed with a specific power of arrest.

9.2 A ban is the ultimate preventive measure[1] and we note that the Government has no desire to see bans being imposed more frequently[2]. Our comments and recommendations reflect our concern that banning orders have been used in recent years with increasing frequency, despite the fact that the overwhelming majority of demonstrations are conducted peacefully and without incident. NCCL policy has for many years opposed general banning orders as a serious infringement of the right of assembly[3]. However, NCCL has recognised that in exceptional circumstances and on grounds of serious public disorder alone there should be a power to ban marches and processions[4], but a power which should be described and executed in the narrowest possible terms and for the shortest possible time[5].

NCCL is becoming increasingly concerned that bans on processions which were almost unknown in the early 1970s have now become commonplace. There were six bans in the period 1974 - 1980 and thereafter 50 to 31st July 1983[6]. In the light of the increasing use of the power to ban marches the NCCL Executive Committee is now considering a policy of outright opposition to all bans.

9.3 *The test*

The present test for banning processions (and also for re-routing them) is the apprehension on reasonable grounds that the procession *may occasion serious public disorder*. Many commentators, including Lord Scarman and the authors of the Green Paper, have suggested that the word 'serious' should be deleted. But the White Paper accepts that the word 'serious' represents a real distinction and an important safeguard. The advantage of the 'serious public disorder' test is that it fits neatly into a wider scheme of public order controls. Its use is less likely to be seen as political than other tests and, generally speaking, if applied properly, it is a stringent test. The serious public disorder test is existing NCCL policy and was supported by the Home Affairs Committee[7].

9.4 An alternative test, supported amongst others by the Commission for Racial Equality, the Trades Union Congress and the Board of Deputies of British Jews, is that a march may be banned only *on the ground that it would incite racial hatred*. It is argued that recent use of the current power to make banning orders has been necessary only in the case of racist marches. The solution accordingly would be to amend section 70 of the Race Relations Act 1976 to include the power to ban any demonstration which is likely to (or intended to) intimidate a racial group, stir up racial hatred or prejudice, or be racially provocative or intimidatory to the community[8]. But against this it is argued that such a proposal would only invite the police to discriminate between racial groups and to be politically selective – such discriminatory bans could only raise street tension. For example, just as incitement to racial hatred charges have been brought against black activists, so National Front marches could be allowed to take place while a black people's march opposing the National Front could be banned. For similar reasons Lord Scarman rejected the proposal that the police should have the power to cancel one demonstration where two opposing parties are planning to march in the same area[9].

9.5 A third alternative is to *remove the power to order bans altogether*. A minority of the Home Affairs Committee said that bans were 'wrong in principle and unnecessary in practice'[10]. The police have powers of re-routing under Section 3 of the Public Order Act and although they should not be used so as to prevent the intended effect of the march, they are sufficient to prevent serious public disorder. In addition, as we have seen, the police have widespread preventive and arrest powers under the existing law. Against this proposal it is argued that by removing the power to make banning orders other police powers to enforce conditions and restrictions would be so rigorously applied that demonstrations would be prevented from carrying out their intended purpose. (This argument applies with considerable force to the Government's proposals on static demonstrations – see Chapter 11 below.) But NCCL takes the view that it is time to give further consideration to opposing all bans. It should be remembered that in 1936 the key proposals of the Public Order Bill and to which most attention was given in Parliament were Clauses 1 and 2 which concerned the wearing of uniforms and the prohibition of quasi-military organisations. Clause 3 (re-routing and banning orders) received modest attention, although NCCL's submission declared outright opposition to bans. The words of that submission still apply today:

'The right to organise processions without the previous consent of the executive is a vitally important democratic liberty and is part of the Rule of Law which, in Dicey's words, is "a striking feature, we might almost say the essential characteristic of the English constitution." The Council are gravely concerned at this attempt to abrogate the Rule of Law by placing a discretionary power to ban processions into the hands of the executive.'

9.6 *Blanket bans*

As the White Paper points out, the problem with blanket bans is that 'the innocent suffer with the guilty'[11]. Section 3 of the Public Order Act provides for orders prohibiting the holding of 'all public processions or any class of public procession'. In practice, the Home Secretary has approved blanket all-purpose bans which were often designed to cover one march only, for example a seventeen-day ban in Grimsby, Hull, Cleethorpes and Scunthorpe in July 1981 to stop a proposed National Front march in Grimsby. 'Class' bans are rarer. One example was the one month ban in Birmingham, Coventry and Solihull in 1974 of any public procession in connection with the death of James McDade, a member of the IRA. NCCL approves of the Government proposal to apply a ban to a single march and *recommends* that the ban of a single named march should be the only form of ban. Despite the danger of selectivity in its application it avoids the use of blanket bans and class bans, for example, of 'processions of a political character' which are unacceptably wide in civil liberty terms and unnecessary in practice to prevent public disorder.

9.7 *Duration of bans*

Section 3 further provides that processions may be banned 'for such period not exceeding three months'. In view of our proposal in paragraph 9.6 this period should be reduced to one month. The power to ban is so serious that any longer period should be justified by renewed application.

9.8 *Notice of bans*

At present Section 3 contains no requirement for the giving of notice of a banning order. This is a necessary requirement in order to give the organisers time to cancel their arrangements and to protect them from prosecution for failing to comply with the

50

banning order[12]. We *recommend* that the Home Secretary should be required to give public notice to the organisers of the existence of a banning order within 72 hours.

9.9 *Procedure for bans*

The White Paper proposes no change in the existing procedure for making banning orders. We feel, however, that there is a significant weakness relating to the procedure in London. Outside London the Chief Constable is required to apply to the borough or district council for an order which must, if approved, be ratified by the Home Secretary[13]. In theory at least this provides an adequate three-tier chain of responsibility including most significantly, the elected local authority acting on behalf of all local interests and, hopefully, involving the police authority for the relevant area. There is certainly a need for local authorities to act as a check on the views of the chief officer of police.

But in London, the Metropolitan Police Commissioner or, where appropriate, the City of London Police Commissioner, applies directly to the Home Secretary[14]. This difference may have arisen because of the anomalous position of Home Secretary as the police authority for London, a position NCCL has consistently argued against by suggesting that there should be an elected police authority for the London area. In line with this policy and with the practice outside London, we *recommend* that the Commissioner should apply first to the local authority, namely the Greater London Council or, when abolished, to the relevant borough council, which may then seek ratification from the Home Secretary. The White Paper's argument against this proposal is that the Home Secretary provides 'the necessary element of local knowledge and political accountability'. The Home Secretary may be accountable to Parliament, but he is not accountable to either the Greater London Council or the London boroughs. Nor is it likely that the Home Secretary has much time to acquire 'local knowledge' of detailed policing matters in London.

An alternative procedure would be to allow the local authority to initiate a ban without waiting for the chief officer of police to seek one, as some local authorities in Scotland are able to do[15]. If bans are to be retained their use must be reduced. However, giving the local authority power to initiate a ban may be seen by some local authorities as encouragement to do so and by others as political interference, whereas the three-tier approach of police, local authority and Home Secretary may be the most effective procedure for reducing the number of bans.

9.10 *Delegation of application for ban*

The White Paper proposes[16] that the power of a Chief Constable to apply for a ban (or impose conditions in advance) is capable of delegation to an Assistant Chief Constable (or in London from the Commissioner to an Assistant Commissioner). NCCL opposes this proposal. The importance of the power to ban has previously been reflected by its exercise at the top level of the police hierarchy. Nothing less will do. In this way the Chief Constable is directly accountable to the police authority and the Home Secretary[17].

9.11 *Right of appeal*

We *recommend* (as we did in 1936) that the organisers of a banned march or procession should have a specific statutory right of appeal to a High Court judge against the making of a banning order. This right is necessary in view of the courts' reluctance to interfere with bans under the existing judicial review procedure[18]. In 1981 NCCL's solicitor acted for the Campaign for Nuclear Disarmament in their challenge to a twenty-eight day ban on all public processions within the Metropolitan Police district (from Radlett to Croydon and from Kenley to Heathrow). Despite the acceptance that CND marches were commonly and peacefully held, the Court of Appeal declined to hold that the ban was wrong or unlawful in any way. The Court could not say that the Commissioner was at fault in making the order, especially when the Home Secretary had agreed with it[19]. This is a clear example of the operation of judicial review. The process does not allow judicial involvement in the merits of the decision itself. It permits only judicial review of whether the decision has been properly reached. Therefore even if the decision is plainly bad (and the court thinks it is bad) it will not reverse the decision unless it can be shown that it was not taken in a proper manner. The process of judicial review – the examination of procedural propriety – is therefore very limited in scope.

9.12 *Offences and powers of arrest*

The proposed new offence of knowingly participating in a prohibited procession (maximum penalty; fine of £400) is unnecessary and a dangerous extension of police public order powers. It is unnecessary because, apart from the considerable range of police powers to disperse crowds, Section 3(4) or the Public Order Act already penalises the organisers or those who assist in the organisation of processions held or intended to be held in contravention of banning orders. It is dangerous because apart from the organisers themselves, there may be many who are unaware or uncertain of the terms of the order, for example, those who arrive at assembly points for a march unaware of the ban and who walk in groups along part of the banned route. These powers which could be exercised in the absence of any disorder at all, could lead to the arrest of innocent demonstrators or alternatively possible serious confrontation inspired by the exercise of the police power. Although the offence includes the element of 'knowingly', this will not prevent arrests taking place. The police will not stop to ask if the particular demonstrator had read in the newspaper that a blanket ban was in force. Nor will the element of 'knowingly' be so easy for the demonstrator, now a defendant, to disprove, particularly if media coverage has been given of the ban but the defendant is unaware of it.

10. MARCHES AND PROCESSIONS – CONDITIONS

10.1 *The new tests*

The Government proposes that the basis for exercising the power to impose conditions on a march or procession should be extended by adding to the present sole test of the apprehension of serious public disorder[1] two further alternative tests of *serious disruption to the local community* and of *the coercion of individuals*. The Government also proposes that the law should be amended to allow the senior police officer present at a march to issue directions.

10.2 NCCL completely opposes these new proposals which lie, together with the new powers to impose conditions on static demonstrations (see Chapter 11 below), at the heart of the Government's strategy. They would give sweeping new powers to police officers in the control and restriction of the right of assembly. They are completely unacceptable and are tantamount, as we shall see below, to preventing the very purpose of a march or procession without actually banning it.

10.3 The new tests of serious disruption to the local community and of the coercion of individuals are not concerned with public disorder, let alone serious public disorder, which has been the standard test since 1936 and which the Government feels is still the appropriate test for bans. The proposals depart from the scope of any plan to curb disorder and as such amount to a deliberate disavowal that marches and processions (and static demonstrations) are a vital and integral part of normal community life in a democratic society.

10.4 Instead of encouraging the peaceful co-operation of authority and protestor, the use of these extensive new police powers would be likely to create resentment and confrontation. The White Paper admits that the formal power to impose conditions under Section 3(1) is rarely used:

> 'The police prefer to discuss the plans for a march with the organisers and to negotiate an informal agreement about the route and other matters. In general these arrangements work well: the Metropolitan Police have given only two examples of cases where they have imposed formal conditions in order to prevent serious disorder in the last five years'[2].

The examples given were of straightforward re-routing. In the Green Paper it was openly admitted that the police used their coercive powers with caution, particularly since resort to formal directions could 'in certain circumstances be regarded as provocative'[3].

In NCCL's view the Government is putting forward a law of confrontation, a stark denial of the need to police a democratic society by consent.

10.5 *Unnecessary proposals*

The proposed new powers are also *unnecessary* under the existing law. In addition to the national powers to ban or re-route marches and processions (under Section 3 of the Public Order Act 1936), the police have wide local powers. In London the Commissioner can make regulations and give directions to keep order and prevent obstruction of the streets.[4] These powers are wider than the Public Order Act powers. In practice they are used to supplement the national powers and to extend them from moving demonstrations to static ones. For example they are often used for sit-down protests. It is also under these powers that the Commissioner makes an order at the start of each Parliamentary session banning all open-air meetings and processions near Westminster on any day when Parliament is sitting. It is an example of how such powers snowball that the control of protest over a wide area within range of Westminster developed out of a desire to give Members of Parliament unobstructed access to the House.

Outside London similar powers are granted in all boroughs and districts[5] and in addition many local authorities pass byelaws covering public meetings held in their area.

10.6 It is therefore remarkable that, in seeking to persuade of the need for more powers, the White Paper makes no reference to these local powers, which are both far-reaching and often not readily available to public scrutiny. NCCL therefore *recommends* that both national and local powers should be rationalised and codified; this is essential for the proper definition of the right of assembly.

10.7 *'Serious disruption to the local community'*

The proposed test of serious disruption to the local community is justifiable, it is argued, on the ground that marches should be prevented from causing unreasonable disruption to local residents, other users of the highway and adjoining shops and premises. In short, the Government proposes nothing less than a test of inconvenience, to be judged, according to the proposal, by the senior officer present. Will the senior officer measuring disruption or inconvenience protect the rights of individuals to assemble and protest? Or will he or she seek to protect all other persons from any disruption, from noise chanted in protest, from traffic jams, from traffic diversions, from temporary obstruction of the pavement, from having to see the protest ('the great unwashed', as one senior officer present recently described a march in Fleet Street) and from having to hear its message?

The range of different types of procession is vast: from the ceremonial religious procession to the mass political march, from the convoy of delegates to official meetings to the small locally-organised protest. Will the police be able to draw distinctions between them on the basis of an arbitrary test of 'disruption'? In 1983 six ceremonial processions necessitated the employment of 1,000 police officers, involving re-routing of traffic and massive disruption of a temporary nature. In future will they also be made the subject of restrictive conditions?

10.8 *'The coercion of individuals'*

The alternative test of the coercion of individuals is also remarkably wide and uncertain. The White Paper ironically promotes it as a 'libertarian safeguard'. It is 'designed to prevent demonstrations whose overt purpose is to persuade people from being used as a cloak by those whose real purpose is to intimidate or coerce'.[6]

What is meant by this is not clear. If by 'coercion' the White Paper means constraint or restraint by force (the usual definition), then the use of force or disorder can properly be controlled by the extensive coercive and arrest powers (set out in Chapter 4 above) without resort to extra pre- or post-conditions. Presumably the White Paper does not mean government by force (another common definition). But if what is meant by 'coercion' is the forceful or vigorous expression of views directed at those who least wish to hear them, like Government, then this proposal has very serious implications, not least in the subjective application of the test by police officers who must first discover the 'overt purpose' of the march or procession and then divine the covert purpose ('cloak') behind it.

10.9 This process is far from satisfactory and is likely to lead to bad policing. Once more it must be said that this is yet another proposal that is unnecessary to prevent or control public disorder. Take the actual example cited by the White Paper. The National Front organise a counter-demonstration to a march by the Troops Out Movement describing their purpose as being to 'stop this vermin. . . don't let them march'. If there is a real likelihood of serious public disorder, the march can under the present law be re-routed or, as a last resort, banned. If offences, of disorder or incitement to racial hatred occur during the march, the police can act. Both the test of serious disruption to the local community and the test of coercion of individuals are likely to thrust the police firmly into the political arena, where their judgments will be seen as either an interference with fundamental freedoms or sufficient provocation for refusal to comply with the conditions imposed.

10.10 *Imposition of conditions*

Which conditions will be imposed if these tests become law? This is yet another question which remains unanswered by the White Paper. The Government's claim that the new tests will not enable the police to ban a procession[7] would not ring true, for example, to journalists or print workers wishing to march down Fleet Street to protest about wages or working conditions when they find out they are to be re-routed to Battersea Park on the grounds that their march will be disruptive to the arrival of the paper lorries at the warehouses or coercive to their employers. And re-routing may not be the only condition imposed on the march. Picking up the exhortation from the Home Affairs Committee that the police should employ existing powers more actively, the Home office has agreed to 'advise' the police that their powers are wider than simply re-routing.[8] Thus, for example, under the Public Order Act 1936 'such conditions as appear (to the Chief Officer of Police) to be necessary for the preservation of public order' may in future include restrictions on numbers and duration (see Chapter 11 below) as well as route. Therefore the show of support for the Fleet Street march could be markedly reduced by police requirements that only six go on the march (six being a number much favoured by the police for pickets).

10.11 *Delegation of the power*

The proposal for the delegation of these powers to the senior officer present is inadequate as a safeguard against abuse. Although there is something to be said for the senior officer present being able to give directions in the event of an unexpected occurrence, in practice the conditions will have been imposed before the march or procession takes place. The decision to restrict fundamental freedoms is, in NCCL's view, so important that it should be made by the Chief Officer of Police and not by an officer of lower rank.

10.12 *Appeal*

NCCL *recommends* that organisers of marches or processions should have statutory right of appeal to a High Court judge against the imposition of conditions. As with appeals against bans, the judicial review procedure has proved inappropriate and ineffective.

10.13 In reconsidering their proposals, the Government would do well to note the words of Lord Denning when Master of the Rolls:

'The right to demonstrate and protest are, like the right of free speech, rights which it is in the public interest that individuals should possess and exercise without impediment, so long as no wrongful act is done.[9]

11. STATIC DEMONSTRATIONS – CONDITIONS

11.1 The White Paper proposes that there should be no new power to ban static demonstrations and no advance notice requirement, but that there should be *a new power to impose conditions on static demonstrations in the open air,* exercisable by reference to the same criteria as are proposed for processions *(serious disruption to the local community* or *the coercion of individuals),* but limited to the *location, numbers and duration* of the demonstration.

11.2 Whilst welcoming the conclusion that no new powers to ban or to require advance notice of static demonstrations are proposed, NCCL rejects as a further wholesale attempt to restrict the freedom of assembly the proposal to enable the police to impose conditions. In our view this is one of the most dangerous proposals in the White Paper.

11.3 The proposals are intended to catch and restrict a wide range of assemblies. These include, according to the White Paper, meetings, counter-demonstrations, outside meetings, demonstrations outside embassies, lobbies of Parliament, pickets and demonstrations in support of pickets. They range from the mass political rally in Trafalgar Square to the modest protest of parents calling for a pedestrian crossing for their children to cross the road safely, from religious services to pop festivals, from the big meeting to a small minority gathering.

11.4 NCCL *recommends* that there should be no restriction on static demonstrations as proposed by the White Paper. We have sought to emphasise repeatedly three principles: the need for legal acceptance of basic rights, the minimum restriction upon the exercise of those rights and the development of co-operation between police and public in the exercise of those rights.

11.5 The proposed tests for imposing conditions on static demonstrations are the same as for marches and processions: the reasonable apprehension of *serious disruption to the local community* or of *the coercion of individuals.* As we have argued above (see Chapter 10) these tests are unacceptably wide and vague. They involve the application of subjective judgement by the police, often in a political context. The exercise of police power in this way will provoke resentment and hostility. A test of disruption to the local community will become a test of convenience and a protest is never convenient to those against whom it is directed. A test of coercion of individuals is undoubtedly aimed at picketing.[1] Every employer whose premises are picketed will call for the police to impose conditions by saying that the picket is disruptive and/or coercive to those seeking to enter the premises. The police will be obliged to act accordingly.

11.6 How will the police act? They will have no power to ban the static demonstration, but they will have the power to do the next best thing:

to impose conditions on the static demonstration in relation to *location, numbers* and *duration*. In many circumstances the restrictions will be tantamount to a ban, a danger which the White Paper foresees, but fails to avoid. Parents protesting outside the Town Hall about inadequate child-care facilities could be removed to the local park, to what the White Paper calls a 'less sensitive area'. Pickets could be reduced to one in number.[2] A proposed assembly at Greenham Common of 10,000 people could be restricted to 50 people for half an hour. The White Paper even suggests that the police should limit the numbers of spectators at football matches.[3] These proposals undermine the necessary level of tolerance of the right of protest required in a free society. What price inconvenience? Will fireworks for a royal wedding, the carnival in Notting Hill, a 24-hour vigil outside South Africa House, a CND protest at Molesworth all fail the test?

11.7 The White Paper also proposes to complete the control of the static demonstration by the creation of *an offence of knowingly failing to comply with police directions or conditions*. This is yet another criminal offence which has marginal bearing on public disorder. Fresh powers are unnecessary as we have repeatedly shown and as the White Paper itself persuasively argues in rejecting special controls for demonstrations outside embassies.

12. PUBLIC MEETINGS

12.1 The Government makes no proposals to alter the law relating to public meetings in closed premises. It recognises that it is neither necessary nor desirable to extend the controls of bans and conditions to meetings in closed premises.

12.2 In broad terms NCCL agrees with this approach. The White Paper recognises that serious public disorder is much less frequently associated with indoor meetings. Existing powers include the offences of endeavouring to break up a public meeting or inciting others to do so under Section 1 of the Public Meeting Act 1980, and causing a disturbance at an election meeting contrary to Section 84 of the Representation of the People Act 1949. These are sufficient powers and require no extension.

12.3 On the contrary consideration should be given to redefining the test set out in both Acts of 'acting in a disorderly manner.' This phrase is widely drawn and may include conduct falling short of words or behaviour requiring police action. Legitimate heckling or boisterous comment should be stifled by action from the chair and the support of the meeting, rather than by police intervention. A more satisfactory test would be based on our proposed public disorder test, which is limited to violence or the immediate threat of violence to persons or property (see para 6.1 above).

12.4 *Access to Election meetings*
Candidates at Parliamentary elections and Local Government elections have the right under Sections 82 and 83 of the Representation of the People Act 1949, to use certain schools and halls for public election meetings free of charge. In the past these special provisions have been exploited to full advantage by organisations like the National Front. Meetings which should have been *genuinely open to the public* have been held behind closed doors with only sympathisers present. Public debate on electoral issues has been replaced by private meetings at public expense.

12.5 The problem hinges on the definition of 'public meeting' which on this issue has not been tested in the courts. Neither the Representation of the People Act nor the Public Meeting Act contains a definition. The Public Order Act 1936 does provide a definition:

> ' "Public meeting" includes any meeting in a public place and any meeting which the public or any section thereof are permitted to attend, whether on payment or otherwise.'

But this definition was created for public order purposes and is clearly too wide for the context of election purposes.

12.6 NCCL therefore *recommends* (in line with our policy since 1979) that 'public meeting' should be redefined for the purposes of the Representation of the People Act 1949 so as to ensure that election meetings are genuinely open to the public. This recommendation will stem concern that candidates who hold what are in effect closed, all-ticket rallies should not enjoy the financial benefit of a room provided by the local authority free of hire charge. In endorsing this proposal (which was not adopted in the White Paper) the Home Affairs Committee[1] recommended that a substantial proportion of seats at election meetings should be open to the public. We therefore propose that 'public meeting' should be defined as follows:

> ' "Public meeting in furtherance of a candidature" means any meeting held under the provisions of Section 82 or Section 83 of this Act and which any person may attend without restriction on entrance by ticket, invitation or otherwise, provided that a candidate or their agent may retain for the candidate's own purposes not more than one quarter of the seats available in the meeting room.'

This definition allows for the attendance, for example, of a local party's executive committee and other supporters. But above the proportion of a quarter of the seats available the meeting must be open to the public on a first come, first served basis. If any political party wishes to hold a meeting to show 'the widespread and national support a candidate enjoys', it should hold a private meeting, at its own expense, to which the press can be invited.

13. POLICE TACTICS

13.1 It is not the intention of this paper to consider police tactics in any depth. But no review of public order law can fail to touch upon some important aspects of this subject.

13.2 *The causes of public disorder*

As we have already indicated (in para 2.6) the White Paper has approached its review without considering the causes of public disorder either in general terms or in specific cases. Much immediate violence has been sparked off by police behaviour of tactics. We have already referred (in para 2.6) to Brixton in 1981, inner city violence in 1985 and the Kerner Commission's conclusions on civil disorders that police behaviour was the most frequently perceived source of grievance in the black community in the USA.

13.3 Police tactics, training and equipment have changed radically over the last ten years, having a dramatic effect on public order events. While NCCL observers at well-conducted demonstrations (the vast majority) report back on constant communications between stewards and senior officers, with well-disciplined ranks, there is another side to the coin. Tactics of aggressive policing, the force of numbers and the wide use of discretionary police powers have caused resentment and sometimes violence amongst protestors.

In 1983 at the Colin Roach demonstrations, there was a high number of arrests and very active policing. In the subsequent court cases police evidence was not accepted on several occasions. In the same year during the NGA Stockport Messenger dispute, there was an inappropriate attempt to use the six picket limitation. In 1985 a difficult problem over the peace convoy's approach to Stonehenge was 'solved' by breaking up the convoy with police violence to persons and property. In the miners' strike demonstrations were very heavily policed. In Sheffield the police over-reacted to an incident outside the Trades Council club. In Mansfield clashes were caused when police controls made dispersal difficult. In London over-restricted access to Parliament led to fighting.

The late summer of 1985 brought violence to inner city streets, with the misuse of police firearms and other police behaviour sparking off local tension.

13.4 The Home Office cannot simply ignore the causes of disorder. Indeed a Home Office research study has looked at the problem but without trying to solve it:

'The crux of the problem is that for a given incident there may not be any happy medium between a weak response undermining the authority and credibility of the police, and one which may provoke more serious violence.'[1]

Recent police tactics, particularly in some areas during the miners' strike, appear to be moving towards a more aggressive and provocative style of policing. Instead of the police complaining that they are unable to obtain convictions in riot cases because the evidence is not good enough, they should be examining their own tactics and the causes of disorder. NCCL's concern about police violence and police handling of protesters is as strong today as it was in 1934 over the handling by the police of the hunger marches and anti-fascist demonstrations.

13.5 *Riot control*

The modern aggressive style of policing is most graphically displayed by the use of riot equipment in quasi-military manoeuvres. Authorised equipment available to police forces now includes short shields, long shields, truncheons, helmets and visors, CS gas (used in Toxteth in 1981 contrary to Home Office guidelines), CR gas, water cannon and plastic bullets[2] – a cylinder 3.25 inches long and 1.5 inches in diameter. Despite the chilling statistic that fourteen people were killed by rubber and plastic bullets in Northern Ireland between 1972 and 1982 (seven of them children) Sir Kenneth Newman, Commissioner of the Metropolitan Police, has 'warned' the people of London that he will not shrink from using plastic bullets 'for restoring peace and preventing crime and injury'. (*The Times*, 8 October 1985).

13.6 Plastic riot shields, first used by the police at Lewisham in 1977, have been used as offensive weapons to hit people. They also prevent police officers being able to see and identify individuals using violence. Protective overalls have covered up the numbers on police uniform and prevented their identification. As NCCL said in evidence[3] to Lord Scarman's inquiry on Brixton, equipment which depersonalises the police and which makes them look like fighting machines increases the likelihood that they will be regarded as legitimate targets for attack.

13.7 A secret manual of riot tactics drawn up by the Association of Chief Police Officers (ACPO) has revealed the violent, if not unlawful, nature of approved police manoeuvres. It describes in detail:

– how 'snatch squads' can run thirty yards into a crowd to arrest 'an identifiable offender'
– how baton charges can disperse crowds

- how a short shield and baton carrying team can 'incapacitate missile throwers and ring leaders by striking in a controlled manner with batons about the arms and legs or torso'
- how mounted police can disperse a crowd 'using impetus and weight to create fear and a scatter effect' by advancing into the crowd at a canter
- how battle cries and the rhythmic beating of shields with truncheons should be used.

13.8 These descriptions give some credence to Ambrose Bierce's definition of a riot in 1906[4] as 'A popular entertainment given to the military by innocent bystanders.' In *NCCL's view*, priority should be given in any riot training to the development of tactics of containing rioters (where there is in fact a serious public order disturbance) in as small an area as possible and of their dispersal with minimum force. The primary aim should be, as counsel to the Red Lion Square inquiry said, 'not to corner and arrest, but to make people move away and to let them get away.' Dispersal to this effect should be preceded by a public announcement telling the crowd to disperse.

13.9 In addition, all instructions and guidelines on riot control tactics should be made public. And NCCL has always opposed the use of gas, plastic or rubber bullets, water cannon and sonic and photic devices.

13.10 *Road blocks*

The police have always had fairly generous statutory powers to stop motor vehicles: to check the name and address of the driver, to search for explosives, drugs and stolen property. The Police and Criminal Evidence Act 1984 provides for local 'road checks' to see whether a vehicle is carrying a criminal offender or an escaped criminal.[5]

13.11 But the police have also been using common law powers to impose roadblocks. A coach containing National Front supporters was stopped from entering Wakefield. Kent miners were stopped at the Dartford tunnel. Many other miners during the dispute were stopped from entering specific localities, particularly in Nottinghamshire.

The basis for the exercise of these powers is that cars and persons should be turned back in order to prevent a possible breach of the peace at their destination. The use of the power has been approved by the High Court on two separate occasions.[6] Thus, the 'intercept policy', the police name for the massive road block operation in Nottinghamshire, was legitimised. Those who disobeyed or queried the instructions were arrested for the offence of obstructing a police officer in the execution of his duty (see para

6.9 above).

13.12 NCCL *condemns* this use of road blocks as an unnecessary restriction on the freedom of movement and as an invasion of privacy. The decisions of the courts have misinterpreted the law, which quite clearly states that the breach of the peace has to be *imminent,* that is proximate in time and place.[7] It creates a dangerous precedent for the police to restrict the movement of protesters. Already it has been used at Molesworth and Stonehenge. The indiscriminate use of road blocks is a tactic which will alienate large numbers of protesters and make policing by consent more difficult.

13.13 *Arrest and bail conditions*

Another development, increasingly reported to NCCL, is the use of large-scale arrests with comparatively few charges. The effect is intimidating. It removes protesters from the place of their intended protest, often without any reference to a proper public disorder test (see para 6.1 above). It threatens them away from future protests. In June 1985, of more than 200 people arrested at a CND demonstration, 80% were released without charge.

13.14 A variation was practised against members of the 'peace convoy' who sought to reach Stonehenge for the summer solstice. Large numbers of people were arrested and charged with the serious offence of unlawful assembly (penalty unlimited). Some six weeks later all charges of unlawful assembly were dropped. This kind of practice is highly intimidatory and also provides an excuse for a further control, *the bail condition.* When the case is brought before the court, the police emphasize the serious nature of the charge, but say that they will not object to bail if stringent bail conditions are imposed. The conditions will prevent the defendant from going to specified places or taking part in specified activities. In the 'peace convoy' cases, this procedure provided the Wiltshire police with a good excuse for moving the problem out of their area.

13.15 *Information gathering*

One feature arising out of police use of road blocks, arrest powers and bail conditions is the process of gathering information on individuals, groups of individuals, organisations, and their movements. The increase of technology and police computer use has made it easy to collect and store information which is of a non-criminal nature. Because of the absence of a Freedom of Information Act, the individual has no right of access to this information, to correct it if inaccurate, or even to know if it exists.

There has only been one case against the police (to the writer's knowledge) in which a judge has made an order that fingerprints, photographs and, most significantly personal information, should be destroyed. This was a case taken up by NCCL in which an innocent man had been arrested under the Prevention of Terrorism Act for attending a terrorist trial at the Old Bailey out of curiosity. A Special Branch officer had admitted to the court that he had told the man that he could write to the Metropolitan Police Commissioner to ask for the return for his fingerprints, even though he knew it was the force's policy to keep them.[8]

13.16 *Police accountability*[9]
The silence of most police authorities over the controversial policing methods adopted during the miners' dispute was rarely broken. Most police authorities are content to rubber stamp the decisions of their chief constables. Very few authorities call for reports on local policing issues. Others pass budgets without controversy.

13.17 The tripartite structure of the police, the Home Office and the police authority[10] ought to provide true accountability. But it has failed to do so. The balance of this structure was seen to break down in the miners' dispute. Police authorities had no power or control over their police forces, whereas the Home Secretary gave national directions with the assistance of the National Reporting Centre. The devolved system of decentralised policing was superseded by a national police force in all but name.

13.18 The balance must be redressed. Police authorities must have powers to ensure that local policing priorities and policies reflect local needs and concerns. They must have greater influence over police expenditure of their ratepayers' money. Parliament also has a role to play: in laying down guidelines for the true working of the tripartiate structure. In this context, accountability means more than just 'giving an account of': it means giving local police authorities an element of control over the police.

14. COSTS OF POLICING DEMONSTRATIONS

14.1 The White Paper calls for comments on a proposal that a *police authority should be able to recover policing costs from the organisers of a demonstration* through civil proceedings where the organisers and participants deliberately flout conditions imposed by the police.[1]

   14.2 This is a compromise proposal, for the White Paper makes it quite clear that the Government would like to go further in its desire to put a price on the right of assembly:

> 'While in no way wishing to inhibit the peaceful and lawful expression of opinion, the Government has considerable sympathy with the views of those who believe that demonstrators should meet all or some of the costs of policing their own demonstrations.'[2]

14.3 NCCL rejects this proposal. It is wrong in principle to place a price on the exercise of basic rights. In practice it would discriminate against the poor (both individuals and organisations), it would raise the spectre of the licensing of demonstrations, it would cause problems of enforcement, and it would encourage bargaining between police and organisers as to how demonstrations should be policed, with what manpower, and at what cost.

   14.4 Enforcement would be difficult (or unfair) either where conditions imposed by the police were flouted by individuals or a breakaway group over whom the organiser had no control, or where there was no clear organiser. In a decided case *(Flockhart v. Robinson[3])* it was held that the organiser can be someone who simply waves and shouts 'follow me'.

   14.5 The assessment of costs (or penalties) and the contribution towards costs where many groups of different sizes had demonstrated together (as at the mass rally against Botha in 1984), would cause lengthy argument and, inevitability, litigation.

   Other difficulties would arise. Would the cost run from the time of the breach of the condition or retrospectively to the commencement of the march, and, if so, would it also include time spent by the police before the march? Many would argue that since demonstrations are often unnecessarily, if not provocatively, over-policed, then the organisers who may have to pay costs should be entitled to a say in the methods of policing. The 1983 Report of the Metropolitan Police Commissioner shows a commendable reduction by 46% compared with 1982 of the manpower commitments for policing public events. NCCL believes that greater consideration should be given to a more economic deployment of personnel and to saving costs, by improving liaison between the police and demonstrators on marches.

14.6 The payment of policing costs undoubtedly needs consideration. Policing at Greenham Common and in the miners' dispute, for example, has placed an excessive burden on local authorities, many of whom have not wanted the invasion into their territory of mass policing. But at the same time there seems to be little sense in the Government's proposal. We wonder if it is seriously considered that Kent miners should be sent a bill for being stopped at the Dartford Tunnel? Will CND have to pay the police and the Ministry of Defence for organising opposition to the Government's nuclear policy? Will anti-racist marches be penalised in costs when a racist organisation breaks up their peaceful protest? We choose these political examples deliberately, because the White Paper seeks to draw a distinction between on the one hand political demonstrations and, on the other hand, assemblies such as the 200,000 gathered at Liverpool airport in 1982 for the Pope's visit, and the march in the same year by the Ad Hoc Committee for Peace in the Falkland Islands. We see no distinction in principle between these gatherings, and we note that the White Paper envisages difficulties in devising criteria which could determine in a satisfactory objective way which assemblies should incur financial charges.

15. FOOTBALL HOOLIGANISM

15.1 The violence at Brussels and at English football clubs, particularly at Birmingham and Luton, in the 1984/1985 season, together with the tragic fire at Bradford in which fifty-six people died, have focused attention on aspects of the game of football which the clubs can no longer ignore. There is nothing new about football hooliganism, but its recent manifestation has shocked football supporters across the world. Many of the clubs facing extinction from dwindling attendances will now have to pass the test of new regulations from the Government, local authorities and themselves in order to win the struggle to survive.

15.2 This Chapter is not intended to support the notion that problems at football matches should be packaged into a special corner of public order law. On the contrary the dangers of that approach should be self-evident. The reduction of freedoms for the sake of special cases has unfortunate precedents in English law, not least in the 'draconian' powers introduced to control terrorism in 1974 after the Birmingham public house bombings. Not only have the 'temporary' provisions of the Prevention of Terrorism Act become permanent, but also some of them have been incorporated into 'normal' police powers. The thin end of the wedge is slowly hammered home.

15.3 It is therefore necessary to see whether some of the current proposals may be particularly harmful to civil liberties, an unnecessary over-reaction to an undoubtedly worrying problem. The proposals come from two main sources: *the White Paper* and *the Popplewell inquiry's interim report (Committee of Inquiry into Crowd Safety and Control at Sports Grounds. Interim Report.* July 1985. Cmnd. 9585.)

15.4 *The White Paper*
The Government has not given undue prominence in the White Paper to football hooliganism. It does, however, deal with the subject on two specific occasions.

i) It proposes[1] *restricting the availability of alcohol* along the lines of Scottish law[2]. This has now been enacted for England and Wales in *The Sporting Events (Control of Alcohol) Act 1985*. This Act is a perfect example of a bad law rushed through Parliament. A similar Private Members Bill[3] fell for lack of support in 1981.

The Act creates for England and Wales new controls over the

sale and possession of alcohol, drunkenness and the sale of certain containers at sports grounds, and drunkenness and the possession of alcohol on certain trains and vehicles carrying passengers to and from sporting events.

The emphasis on drink and drunkenness, although convenient, may be misplaced. Much of the trouble at Birmingham was caused by those who had been drinking outside the ground and who had difficulty getting in when they arrived late. Moderate drinking inside grounds will always be preferable to 'stoking up' at great speed before the match. Many spectators will regret losing the opportunity of have a drink at the leisure activity of their choice. It is unlikely that the Home Secretary will designate racehorse meetings for the purposes of the Act, while attempts in the House of Lords debate to create exemptions for executive boxes was itself an unseemly spectacle. In any event prohibition will not solve the problem. It is of course an offence to be drunk in a public place[4] (which includes football grounds) and to be drunk and disorderly.[5] But already many of the clubs are getting round the intention of the Act by applying for exemptions for all or certain bars, to the local Magistrates' Court.

Concern must be expressed about the new offence of possessing a controlled container.[6] Under the Bill as originally drafted it would have been an offence to take into a football ground any bottle, can or other portable container designed to carry liquid and which is capable of causing injury to a person struck by it, except a medicine bottle. In other words you could no longer take a thermos or a mug. But after backbench Conservative pressure, the Bill was amended to include only disposable containers. However, innocent persons will be at risk of arrest and prosecution for this offence, which carries a penalty of three months' imprisonment. They will be guilty if they carry, for example, a milk carton or soft drinks can or fruit juice container. Under the existing law it is an offence to carry any such item (as with any item capable of being used as a missile – see para 15.5 below) only when it is *intended* to be used as an offensive weapon. The new Act removes the necessity for proof of that intent.

ii) The Government also proposes[7] to bring *missile throwing* within the new extended Section 5 of the Public Order Act 1936, offence (see para 5.2 above). This proposal originates from the Law Commission's draft Bill to codify the criminal law,[8] and from suggestions by senior police officers that it can be difficult at football matches to find appropriate offences with which to charge those picking up and throwing missiles, in circumstances where the injury or damage caused by particular missiles cannot be identified.

Simple though this proposal sounds, it is unfortunately the product of yet another misunderstanding of existing public order law, regrettably a recurrent feature of the Government's thinking in the White Paper.

a) Firstly, the courts have found little difficulty in identifying offences for missile throwers. The Section 5 offence has been widely used. A missile thrower is clearly guilty, under Section 5, of threatening behaviour likely to cause a breach of the peace.

b) Secondly, the use of Section 5 is in any event unnecessary. As we have argued above (see para 6.1) the only acceptable standard for criminal offences in a public order context is the use of violence or the immediate threat of violence to persons or property (the public disorder test). A missile thrower falls into this category, and the law already provides a number of clear offences. If injury is caused the offence committed is an assault (the particular charge will depend on the gravity of the injury). If the missile falls short, it is punishable as an attempted assault. If the injury caused by particular missiles cannot be identified, the offence is still assault, because there is at the very least a threat of assault, which is embraced by the definition of assault. Alternatively, and perhaps more simply, the missile thrower is guilty of possessing an offensive weapon. If damage is caused or intended or threatened the offence is criminal damage (for further explanation of these offences, see Chapter 4 above).

Thus the example provided by the White Paper to illustrate the alleged loophole in the law (the example is taken from the Law Commission's report), namely 'throwing at or towards a person a missile of a kind capable of causing injury which does not hit or falls short', is misconceived. It illustrates both the offences of attempted assault and of possessing an offensive weapon.

c) Thirdly, the real problem for police and prosecutors is not, and never has been, the identification of offences but the identification of offenders. While some senior police officers, such as Mr Peter Wright, the Chief Constable of South Yorkshire, and the man at the centre of the controversial riot trials (see para 5.10 above), have called for a new missile throwing offence, others have concentrated on the use of modern techniques to pick out offenders in crowds. The introduction of video cameras has already proved successful.

72

For example, two offenders were gaoled after being identified on a video film of last season's fixture between Birmingham City and Leeds United[9]. It was also a notable feature of that case that, once identified by clear evidence, the two defendants pleaded guilty to their crimes – of assault, criminal damage and threatening behaviour (for throwing coins). There is an argument that the use of video film may also reduce the risk of police officers picking out the wrong person in the crowd.

15.5 *The Popplewell inquiry*

It is to be hoped that Mr Justice Popplewell will look again at some of his recommendations in the interim report of his inquiry into the events at Bradford City and Birmingham City on the same day. There are three aspects of particular civil liberty concern.

i)   *The creation of new offences*

Throwing missiles – We have already demonstrated that no new offence is needed to deal with missile throwers (see para 15.4(ii) above).

Possessing smoke bombs or similar devices – The possession of a canister containing CS or a similar gas is usually prosecuted as a prohibited weapon under the Firearms Act 1968[10]. Smoke bombs may fall into this category or be prosecuted as an offensive weapon if used or intended for use as a weapon of offence for causing injury. But if the item is not used but is just carried, the simplest solution may be to refuse admission or to remove the person from the ground. No new police power is required for this.

Chanting obscene or racialist slogans – Section 5A of the Public Order Act 1936 penalises conduct likely to stir up racial hatred. We welcome the Government's proposal to extend Section 5A to include conduct intended to stir up racial hatred (see para 7.2 above). Rather than create new offences of limited application, the present law should be properly and more effectively applied. In fact the practical problem is that the police are unwilling to enter packed areas in order to arrest perhaps dozens of spectators chanting together. The creation of 'football' offences is not going to solve this problem. Obscene slogans fall within the Section 5 offence – abusive or insulting words or behaviour likely to cause a breach of the peace. A slogan offence would therefore be an unnecessary extension of the new law, which is itself already too broad, and NCCL has always deplored the duplication of offences. It may also be wrong to penalise this kind of behaviour (except of the racist kind) where there is no violence or immediate threat of violence. Unacceptable behaviour in a public place which is governed by both public order law and private regulation, should in most cases· be dealt with by removal of offenders from the ground.

Running onto a football or sports pitch – The Report calls for further consideration of an offence of running onto a sports pitch. In our evidence to the Popplewell inquiry, we have made it clear that NCCL is wholly against this proposal. Spectators often run on to the pitch to avoid violence on the terraces or in the stands. It may be the only way of escape. More often, pitch invasions are prompted by boisterous spirits rather than criminal intent. In our view they should not be penalised by the criminal law. Should the regaining of the Ashes have been heralded by mass arrest or joyous celebration? If violence or threats of violence to persons or property (NCCL's public disorder test) occur, there are appropriate charges to be made (see Chapter 4 above). Otherwise ejection from the premises under the terms of the spectator-club contract is an adequate and proper response.

ii) *Search before entry*

This would be an unprecedented power, akin to Prevention of Terrorism Act powers and Northern Ireland legislation, and would greatly extend the newly increased stop and search powers in the Police and Criminal Evidence Act 1984.

In the 1984 Act the concept of reasonable suspicion before search – for illegal drugs, stolen goods, firearms, items connected with terrorism, *and* prohibited articles including offensive weapons (a new power)[11] – is retained. But under the Popplewell proposal no reasonable suspicion is required. NCCL has consistently argued against the use of stop and search powers.[12] Even with a 'reasonable suspicion' safeguard this has been one of the most contentious activities of the police, which, although resulting in only a small number of charges, has done more to worsen relations between the police and certain sections of society than any other power. These are 'hunch' powers, often exercised arbitrarily and without foundation. Where there is genuine 'reasonable suspicion', an arrest should be made. This would dramatically reduce the number of unnecessary stops, and would provide an aggrieved person with clearer remedies in the civil courts.

Accordingly, NCCL objects to this proposal both in principle and in practice. It extends the law of stop and search beyond its already considerable limits, and its exercise will inevitably be arbitrary and selective.

Further, the potential for friction is great. Lengthy, random searches will slow down the already frustratingly slow entry to some grounds. Moreover, those who have been drinking up to the last minute outside the ground may let their frustration turn to anger and violence. The proposed power may bring about the very trouble which it is designed to prevent.

iii) *Additional powers of arrest* – The interim report recommends a new power of arrest under the Public Order Act 1936 to apprehend hooligans at a later date in cases where offences have been filmed on closed-circuit television. This is another unnecessary power. The Police and Criminal Evidence Act 1984 provides for arrest by a constable at any time in the case of arrestable offences[13] (including serious assaults and criminal damage), and for lesser offences (including criminal assault and possessing an offensive weapon) the Act provides a power of arrest when the service of a summons is impracticable or inappropriate.[14] In most cases the use of the summons procedure, calling the defendant to court on a particular date, is sufficient, particularly for minor offences and where the defendant has a known, fixed address. But if the suspect refuses to give a name and address, or gives cause for belief that it is false, the Act provides the constable with an arrest power. Therefore the proposal in the Popplewell report for a completely new power of arrest is wholly unnecessary. Instead of simplifying a complicated area of the law, it will cause confusion and uncertainty by piling one police power on top of another.

15.6 *Conclusion*

The problem of violence at or near football grounds is a serious one. But panic measures which infringe the rights of the vast majority of peaceful spectators are not the answer. It might be helpful to try to isolate the causes of football hooliganism – although neither the Government nor the Popplewell inquiry seem to have attempted this. But the attempt to develop a rational, consistent law of public order will not be assisted by the creation of excessive, piecemeal and often unnecessary laws out of short-term, political demands – which appears to be the approach so far.

16. SUMMARY OF NCCL'S CONCLUSIONS

1. NCCL makes six general criticisms of the Government's approach to its review of public order law –
i) The White Paper fails to start from the correct standpoint (para 2.3).
ii) The White Paper fails to provide any legal framework for the right of peaceful assembly (para 2.4).
iii) The White Paper fails to recommend codification of public order law (para 2.5).
iv) The White Paper fails to consider the causes of public disorder (para 2.6).
v) The White Paper proposes an unnecessary and undesirable extension of police powers (para 2.7).
vi) The White Paper's proposals will defeat the very purposes of the review: the prevention of disorder (para 2.8).
2. The law relating to public order should be codified. The overall approach to codification should be founded on the need to protect fundamental freedoms, and should have as its secondary purpose the prevention of public disorder (para 2.9).
3. The structure of the new code should incorporate several key elements consistent with the above approach (para 2.9).
4. The majority of the Government's proposals should be rejected as inconsistent with the above approach. Many of the specific proposals are unacceptable to a free and democratic society and will lead to restraints on the basic freedoms of peaceful assembly and free speech (para 2.9).
5. There should be a positive right to demonstrate (para 3.2). A right of peaceful assembly, including a right to picket, having priority over other legal rights such as the right of passage along the highway, should be enacted (paras 3.2 – 3.14).
6. The offence of obstruction of the highway should be more narrowly defined (para 3.16).
7. The law relating to street collections, leafletting and selling newspapers should be rationalised, simplified and codified as part of a new legal framework of the right of assembly and the use of the highway (para 3.17).
8. NCCL welcomes the proposed abolition of the common law offences of riot, rout, unlawful assembly and affray, but opposes the proposal to replace them with a new range of statutory offences (para 4.2).

9. NCCL makes four broad criticisms of the Government's proposals on public order offences –

i) The White Paper fails to review public order offences in conjunction with police preventive powers (para 4.4).

ii) The White Paper fails to carry out a comprehensive review of public order offences (para 4.7).

iii) The proposed new offences are unnecessary because of existing offences (para 4.8).

iv) The White Paper fails to recommend codification of public order offences (para 4.9).

10. There should be no new offence of failing to disperse after a lawful warning is given ('reading the Riot Act') (para 5.2).

11. The proposed new offence of riot is unnecessary (para 5.4). The proposed definition is wordy, lengthy and difficult to follow (para 5.3). Defendants should be charged with specific criminal acts or not at all (para 5.5).

12. The proposed offence of violent disorder is too wide and too uncertain. As defined it is unnecessary because it overlaps with specific offences of violence or threats of violence to persons or property (para 5.17).

13. Similarly, the proposed new offence of affray is covered by specific criminal offences (para 5.19). It should not be used to circumvent 'evidential difficulties' (para 5.20).

14. The offence of threatening, abusive or insulting words or behaviour etc. contrary to Section 5 of the Public Order Act 1936, should be repealed (as NCCL proposed in 1936) (para 5.22). The proposed extensions to the existing offence are wrong in principle (para 5.25).

15. The proposed offence of disorderly words or conduct should not be implemented. It is dangerously wide and will encompass trivial behaviour which should not be penalised by the criminal law (para 5.30).

16. The proposal to use alternative verdicts should be rejected (para 5.32).

17. The sole criterion for public order controls should be a minimum test of actual violence or immediate threat of violence to persons or property (para 6.1).

18. The wide range of police preventive powers should be simplified and codified (para 6.2). The sole test for any preventive power should be a public disorder test confined to actual violence to persons or property or the threat of violence to persons or property (para 6.3).

19. The police power to take a person before a magistrates' court to be bound over should be abolished (para 6.5).

20.   No public order offence should be expressed in terms wider than our proposed public disorder test of actual violence or immediate threats of violence to persons or property. The existing laws of assault, criminal damage and offensive weapons are sufficient to comply with this test and for the conviction and punishment of offenders (para 6.7).

21.   The offence of obstructing a police officer in the execution of his duty should be restricted to physical obstruction (para 6.9).

22.   The powers relating to the carrying of offensive weapons should be amalgamated (para 6.11).

23.   The offence of intimidation including watching and besetting should be abolished (para 6.13).

24.   NCCL welcomes the proposal to strengthen the offence of incitement to racial hatred by additionally penalising conduct intended to stir up racial hatred (para 7.2) and by removal of the exemption for publication or distribution to members of an association (para 7.3). NCCL also welcomes the proposed new offence of possessing racially inflammatory material with a view to distribution or publication (para 7.7).

25.   NCCL believes that the offence of incitement to racial hatred should be further strengthened, by adding a power of arrest (para 7.4), by removing the Attorney General's consent to prosecution (para 7.5), and by extending the offence to broadcasting (para 7.6).

26.   There should be no requirement to give advance notice of marches and processions (para 8.2).

27.   In exceptional circumstances and on grounds of serious public disorder alone there should continue to be a power to ban marches and processions. The power to ban should be described and executed in the narrowest possible terms and for the shortest possible time. However, NCCL is giving further consideration to a policy of outright opposition to bans (para 9.2).

28.   If the power to ban is to be retained, it should be limited to a single named march or procession. There should be no blanket bans or class bans (para 9.6).

29.   If the power to ban a march or procession is to be retained, the maximum duration of the ban should be one month, not three months (para 97), and notice of the ban should be given within 72 hours (para 9.8). The procedure in London should be altered so as to follow the procedure for the rest of the country (para 9.9). The power to apply for a ban should not be delegated by the chief constable (para 9.10).

30.   There should be a statutory right of appeal to a High Court Judge against an order to ban a march or procession (para 9.11).

31. There should be no new offence of knowingly participating in a prohibited procession (para 9.12).

32. The power to impose conditions on marches and processions should not be extended from the test of apprehension of serious public disorder to two further alternative tests of serious disruption to the local community and of the coercion of individuals (para 10.2).

33. National and local powers to impose conditions on marches and processions should be rationalised and codified within the context of positive rights (para 10.11)

34. There should be no delegation of the power to impose conditions on marches and processions from the chief constable to an officer of lower rank (para 10.11).

35. There should be a statutory right of appeal to a High Court judge against the imposition of conditions on marches and processions (para 10.12).

36. There should be no power to impose conditions on static demonstrations in the open air (para 11.2), and no offence of knowingly failing to comply with police directions or conditions (para 11.7).

37. Access to election meetings should be genuinely open to the public (para 12.4). Accordingly, 'public meeting' should be redefined for election purposes (para 12.6).

38. NCCL is as concerned about police violence and police tactics in 1985 as it was in 1934 (para 13.4).

39. Priority should be given in situations of serious public disorder to containing the disorder and allowing dispersal with minimum force (para 13.8).

40. Instructions and guidelines on police riot control tactics should be made public (para 13.9).

41. The police should not use gas, plastic or rubber bullets, water cannon, or sonic and photic devices (para 13.9).

42. NCCL condemns the use of road blocks 'to prevent a breach of the peace' (para 13.12).

43. Arrest powers, criminal charges and requests for bail conditions should not be used as a tactic to intimidate protestors (paras 3.13 and 13.14).

44. Information gathering in a public order context must be controlled (para 13.15).

45. The balance of the tripartite structure of police accountability must be redressed in order to give police authorities an element of control over their police forces (para 13.18).

46. A police authority should not be able to recover policing costs from the organisers of a demonstration through civil pro-

ceedings, even where the organisers or participants have deliberately flouted conditions imposed by the police (para 14.3).

47.   The use of panic measures in an attempt to deal with football hooliganism will not help the development of a rational, consistent law of public order (para 15.6).

FOOTNOTES

1. INTRODUCTION

1. Cmnd. 9510.
2. See generally Lilly *'The National Council for Civil Liberties – The First Fifty Years'* (Macmillan 1984) and Cox *'Civil Liberties in Britain'* (Penguin 1975).
3. See, eg., *Kent v. Metropolitan Police Commissioner* 'The Times Law Report' 14 May 1981.
4. See generally NCCL publications.

2. THE GOVERNMENT'S APPROACH

1. Cmnd. 9510.
2. *'Review of the Public Order Act 1936 and related legislation'*. Cmnd. 7891.
3. *'The Law Relating to Public Order'*. House of Commons 756 I and II, 7 August 1980.
4. Working Paper No. 82 (1982).
5. HC85, Law Com. No. 123 (1983).
6. Cmnd. 5919 (1975).
7. Cmnd. 8427 (1981).
8. Paras. 1.7 and 1.8.
9. Para. 6.13.
10. Cf the Luxulyan case – *R. v. Chief Constable of Devon and Cornwall, Ex parte Central Electricity Generating Board* [1982] 1 QB 458 – in which the chief constable wished to take no action against protestors.
11. As cited in Brownlie's *'The Law Relating to Public Order'*, 1st Edn. p.21.
12. See Scarman on Brixton paras. 8.8-8.15.
13. Report of the National Advisory Commission on Civil Disorders (1968); and for further discussion see *'Public Disorder'*, Home Office Research Study No 72.

3. POSITIVE RIGHTS

1. Para 1.8.
2. [1976] 1QB 142
3. Cmnd. 5919 (1975).
4. [1936] 1KB 318 at 221.
5. See note 4.
6. [1961] 1WLR 162.
7. Judgment 11 February 1985.
8. Judgment 1 February 1985. (CO/618/84).

9.   See note 2.
10. The Times Law Report 29 November 1984.
11. *'The Guardian'* 21 March 1984.
12. Red Lion Square Report para 5.
13. White Paper para 5.13.
14. Para 5.14.
15. For an excellent brief account see Blake, 'Picketing, Justice and the Law' in *'Policing the Miners' Strike',* edited by Fine and Millar, Lawrence & Wishart and the Cobden Trust (1985).
16. Not the *Rookes v. Barnard* (1964) AC 1129 variety.
17. *Thomas v. NUM* – see note 7.
18. At pp. 25-26 of the approved judgment.
19. See note 2.
20. At p. 177.
21. *Amalgamated Food Employees v. Logan Valley Plaza* 391US308 (1968).
22. Cmnd. 3623, para 875.
23. *Waite v. Taylor* – see note 8.
24. An offence contrary to Section 137(1), Highways Act 1980, which provides:
     If a person without lawful authority or excuse in any way wilfully obstructs the free passage along a highway, he is guilty of an offence and liable to a fine.
25. Pages 3-4, transcript of the approved judgment. Cf. *Hubbard v. Pitt* at p. 174 (per Lord Denning MR).
26. See *Nagy v. Weston* [1964] 1 WLR 280.
27. See Section 5, Police, Factories, etc. (Miscellaneous Provisions) Act 1916 and Street Collections (Metropolitan Police District) Regulations 1979; House to House Collections Act 1939.
28. See *'ACLU News'* May 1985 p.3.
29. See Sieghart, *'The International Law of Human Rights'* (Oxford University Press, 1983) p. 331 note 13.

4.   PUBLIC ORDER OFFENCES – INTRODUCTION

1.   See *R. v. Howell* [1982] QB 416.
2.   Under the Justices of the Peace Act 1361.
3.   Stone's *'Justices Manual'* [1985] para 1-45. And see *Thomas v. Sawkins* [1935] 2 KB 249; *Marshall v. Tinnelly* [1937] 81 Sol. Jo. 902.
4.   Section 3(1).
5.   See Brownlie *'Law of Public Order and National Security'* (2nd edn. Butterworths, 1981) p. 329 note 16.
6.   Ibid. at p. 328 notes 9-12.
7.   Section 137, Highways Act 1980.
8.   Section 51, Police Act 1964.
9.   White Paper paras 2.2 and 6.13.
10. 14th Report, *'Offences against the Person',* Cmnd. 7844, para 159.
11. Codification and rationalisation is proposed in the 14th Report.
12. Law Com No 143, 'Codification of the Criminal Law', HC 270.

5. PUBLIC ORDER OFFENCES – THE GOVERNMENT'S PROPOSALS

1. Working Paper para 2.22.
2. Ibid.
3. *R. v. Caird and Others* (1970) 54 Cr. App. R. 499 at 511.
4. See Working Paper para 2.39. – *R. v. Los 'Daily Telegraph'* 21 October 1981.
5. For the arguments against the offence see Scarman on Brixton at para 7.39.
6. Para 4.2.
7. Scarman on Brixton, para 7.39.
8. Para 3.16.
9. Para 6.4
10. See Working Paper p. 90.
11. Para 5.11.
12. D.G.T. Williams, *'Keeping the Peace'* (1967) p. 239.
13. At para 5.11.
14. See, however, *R. v. Harrow Justices, Ex parte Osaseri*, 'The Times Law Report' 13 July 1985 for restrictions on mode of trial and penalty.
15. Although some restriction has been put on the word 'intimidation' – see Archbold's *'Criminal Pleading, Evidence and Practice'*, 41st Edn. para 19-250.
16. For a full account of the trial see Kettle and Hodges, *'Uprising!'* (Pan) at p. 34 et seq.
17. 19 July 1985.
18. See *'The Times'* 19 July 1985.
19. See e.g. the Luxulyan case: per Denning MR at p. 976 and per Lawton LJ at p.978.
20. See *Kamara v. DPP* [1973] 2 AER 1242; and the abolition of conspiracy to trespass by the Criminal Law Act 1977.
21. See *'The Times'* 4 December 1973.
22. White Paper para 3.13.
23. Law Commission Working Party para 4.2.
24. At para 3.15.
25. *Attorney-General's Reference (No 6 of 1980)* [1981] 3 WLR 125.
26. *Button v. DPP* [1966] AC 591.
27. As the Law Commission suggests at para 3.5.
28. A. Dickey (1971) Crim. LR 265.
29. White Paper para 3.8.
30. (1982) 75 Cr. App. R. 211.
31. [1983] QB 92.
32. (1973) 57 Cr. App. R. 538 at 541.
33. Para 3.26.

6. PUBLIC ORDER OFFENCES – THE ALTERNATIVE APPROACH

1. (1982) QB 416 at 427.
2. At p.471: 'There is a breach of the peace whenever a person who is

lawfully carrying out his work is unlawfully and physically prevented by another from doing it.'

3. See '*The Guardian*' 21 March 1984, *Moss v. McLachlan*, 'The Times Law Report' 29 November 1984, and activity by the Wiltshire police over the 'peace convoy'.
4. At p. 426.
5. Section 115(3), Magistrates' Courts Act 1980.
6. As suggested by the Law Commission for its proposed offence of conduct intended or likely to cause fear or provoke violence – para 5.50.
7. See Law Commission para 5.51.
8. See *Marsh v. Arscott* (1982) 75 Cr. App. R211 and *Parkin v. Norman* (1983) QB92.
9. Section 51, Police Act 1964.
10. (1936) I KB 218.
11. See Brownlie p.18.
12. Ibid, p.20.
13. *Piddington v. Bates* (1960) 3 AER 660.
14. Prevention of Crime Act 1953 and Section 4, Public Order Act 1936.
15. Scarman on Brixton para 7.39.
16. Section 7, Conspiracy and Protection of Property Act 1875.
17. *Galt v. Phipps* (1984)

7. INCITEMENT TO RACIAL HATRED

1. *R. v. Britton* (1967) 2 QB 51.
2. Section 5A[5].
3. Para 99.

8. MARCHES AND PROCESSIONS

1. Para 5.4.
2. Para 130.
3. Para 7.45.
4. Home Affairs Committee Report, para 32.
5. Scarman on Red Lion Square paras 128 and 129.
6. Letter to the Home Secretary, 28 June 1985.

9. MARCHES AND PROCESSIONS – BANS

1. Green Paper para 5.9.
2. Ibid.
3. AGM 1950 and 1951
4. AGM 1951
5. Executive Committee 1980.
6. Hansard February 1984 Vol. 55 Col. 102.
7. Paras 42 and 51.
8. See, e.g. Jim Driscoll's discussion paper on Public Order (February 1985).
9. Scarman on Red Lion Square, para 134[8].
10. Minority report para 21.

11. Para 4.14.
12. Section 3(4), Public Order Act 1936.
13. Section 3(2).
14. Section 3(3).
15. Under the Burgh Police (Scotland) Act 1892 and local legislation.
16. Para 4.28.
17. Section 3, Public Order Act 1936.
18. See Green Paper para 55 for a discussion of this topic.
19. 'The Times Law Report' 14 May 1981.

10. MARCHES AND PROCESSIONS – CONDITIONS.

1. Under Section 3(1), Public Order Act 1936.
2. Para 4.19.
3. Para 61.
4. Section 52, Metropolitan Police Act 1839.
5. See Section 21, Town Police Clauses Act 1847 and Section 171, Public Health Act 1875.
6. Para 4.23.
7. White Paper para 4.25.
8. White Paper Para 4.26.
9. *Hubbard v. Pitt* (1976) IQB 142 at p.177.

11. STATIC DEMONSTRATIONS – CONDITIONS

1. See para 5.7.
2. For picketing generally see Chapter 3 above.
3. Para 5.7.
4. Para 5.12.

12. PUBLIC MEETINGS

1. Para 84.

13. POLICE TACTICS

1. 'Public Disorder', Study no. 72 at p.18.
2. See Gifford, *'Death on the Streets of Derry'* (NCCL 1982)
3. *'Civil Disorder and Civil Liberties'* (NCCL 1981).
4. The Devil's Dictionary.
5. Section 4.
6. Dartford Tunnel case and *Moss v. McLachlan* 'The Times Law Report', 29 November 1984.
7. *R. v. Howell* (1982) QB 416.
8. *'The Times'* 25 April 1980.
9. For a detailed discussion of police accountability see Spencer, *'Called to Account'* (NCCL 1985) and Spencer, *'Police Authorities during the Miners's Strike'* (Cobden Trust 1985).
10. See the Police Act 1964.

14. COSTS OF POLICING DEMONSTRATIONS

1. Para 6.19.

2.   Para 6.16.
3.   [1950] 2KB 498.

15.   FOOTBALL HOOLIGANISM

1.   Para 6.20
2.   Part V, Criminal Justice (Scotland) Act 1980.
3.   The Football Grounds (Control) Bill 1981.
4.   Section 12, Licensing Act 1872.
5.   Section 91, Criminal Justice Act 1967.
6.   Section 2.
7.   Para 3.12.
8.   Clause 8.
9.   *'The Guardian'* 14 August 1985
10. Section 5(1)(b).
11. Section 1.
12. Submission of NCCL to Royal Commission on Criminal Procedure (1979).
13. Section 24(6).
14. Section 25(1).

Appendix 1 GOVERNMENT'S OWN SUMMARY OF ITS WHITE PAPER PROPOSALS

The Government would particularly welcome comments on the proposals marked with an asterisk.

Common Law Public Order Offences

1. The common law public order offences of riot, rout, unlawful assembly and affray should be abolished (paragraph 3.3).

2. Section 5 of the Public Order Act 1936 should be amended to cover conduct intended or likely to cause fear of unlawful violence or to provoke the use of unlawful violence, and should apply in all places except for private dwelling houses (paragraphs 3.8—3.11).

3. There should be a statutory offence of violent disorder which would catch those using or threatening unlawful violence to persons or property in a group of three or more (paragraphs 3.13—3.14).

4. There should be a statutory offence of affray penalising those threatening or using unlawful violence (paragraph 3.15).

5. There should be a statutory offence of riot which would catch those using unlawful violence in a group of twelve or more using or threatening such violence with a common purpose (paragraphs 3.16—3.18).

6.* In the statutory scale of offences all the lesser offences should be available as alternative verdicts to any of the more serious charges. Consideration should be given to making general provision for alternative verdicts in magistrates courts without separate informations having to be laid (paragraph 3.19).

7. The maximum penalties on indictment for these offences should be ten years for riot, five years for violent disorder and three years for affray (paragraph 3.20).

8.* There should perhaps be a new offence of disorderly conduct to catch those who behave in an abusive, insulting, threatening or disorderly manner, causing people to be substantially alarmed, harassed or distressed (paragraphs 3.12—3.26).

9. The Riot (Damages) Act 1886 should remain in being but claims should be subject to the test of the new statutory offence of riot (paragraph 3.27).

10. Certain obsolete statutes relating to public order should be

repeated (paragraph 3.28).

11.   There should be national requirement, with a related offence of non-compliance, for organisers to give advance notice of a march or procession seven days before the event, or as soon as reasonably practicable thereafter. There would be an exemption for processions of a religious, educational or ceremonial character customarily held (paragraphs 4.2—4.6).

12.   The sole ground for the prohibition of processions under section 3 of the Public Order Act should continue to be the apprehension of serious public disorder (paragraphs 4.8—4.11).

13.   In addition to the existing provision for 'blanket' bans, there should be a power to ban a single march or procession (paragraphs 4.12—4.14).

14.   There should be no change to the existing procedure for making banning orders, involving Chief Constables, local authorities and the Home Secretary (paragraph 4.15).

15.   There should be an offence of knowingly participating in a prohibited procession (paragraph 4.16).

16.   The basis for exercising the power to impose conditions on a march or procession should be extended by adding to the present sole test of the apprehension of serious public disorder, those of serious disruption to the local community or the coercion of individuals (paragraphs 4.17—4.25).

17.   Section 3(1) should be amended to allow the senior police officer present at a march to issue directions under the section (paragraph 4.27).

18.   The power to impose conditions in advance of a march or procession or to apply for a ban should be capable of delegation from a chief constable to an assistant chief constable, and from the Commissioner of Police of the Metropolis to an Assistant Commissioner (paragraph 4.28).

19.   There should be a specific power of arrest for offences under section 3(4) of the Public Order Act 1936 and for the proposed new offence of knowingly participating in a prohibited procession (paragraph 4.29).

20.   Section 3(4) should be amended to distinguish between those who disobey police directions on a march and those who organise or incite others to do so (paragraph 4.30).

Static Demonstrations and Meetings

21.   There should be no new power to ban static demonstrations (paragraph 5.3).

22. There should be no advance notice requirement for static demonstrations or assemblies (paragraph 5.4).

23. There should be a new power to impose conditions on static demonstrations in the open air, exercisable by reference to the same criteria as are proposed for processions, but limited to the location, numbers and duration of the demonstration (paragraphs 5.5–5.14).

24. The offence of intimidation in section 7 of the Conspiracy and Protection of Property Act 1875 should carry a specific power of arrest and should have an increased maximum penalty of six months' imprisonment or a fine of £2,000 (paragraphs 5.15—5.16).

25. There should be no change in the substantive law relating to meetings in closed premises (paragraph 5.17).

Miscellaneous matters

26. The provisions in section 4 of the Public Order Act and section 1 of the Prevention of Crime Act 1953 about possessing an offensive weapon should be consolidated (paragraph 6.3).

27. The offence of incitement to racial hatred contained in section 5A of the Public Order Act should be re-cast to penalise conduct *intended* to stir up racial hatred as well as that *likely* to do so (paragraph 6.6).

28. The exemption in section 5A for material published or distributed within an association should be removed (paragraph 6.7).

29. There should be a new offence of *possessing* racially inflammatory material *with a view to distribution or publication*, with related police powers of search, seizure and forfeiture in respect of offending material (paragraphs 6.8—6.9).

30. The offence of incitement to racial hatred should not at present be extended to broadcasting (paragraphs 6.10—6.12).

31. Police common law powers in relation to public order, including the power to disperse an unlawful assembly, should not be codified (paragraphs 6.13—6.15).

32.* The possibility should be explored of introducing a power to enable a police authority to recover policing costs from the organisers through civil proceedings where conditions imposed by the police on a demonstration had been breached (paragraphs 6.16—6.19).

33. Restrictions on the availability of alcohol at or on the way to football matches should be introduced in England and Wales on similar lines to the provisions in Part V of the Criminal Justice (Scotland) Act 1980 (paragraph 6.20).

Application of Proposals in Scotland

34.   The Scottish common law public order offences should not at present be altered, pending the report of the Scottish Law Commission (paragraph 7.4).

35.   The common law police powers should not be codified (paragraph 7.4).

36.   Section 5 of the Public Order Act should be repealed in its application to Scotland (paragraph 7.5).

37.   The changes proposed to section 7 of the Conspiracy and Protection of Property Act 1875 and to section 5A of the Public Order Act should apply in Scotland (paragraph 7.6).

38.   In view of the provisions in the Civic Government (Scotland) Act 1982 for regulating processions, section 3(2) of the Public Order Act should be repealed in relation to Scotland (paragraph 7.9).

39.   There should be a minor amendment to section 62 of the Civic Government (Scotland) Act to require those giving advance notice of a procession to inform not just the local authority but also the chief constable (paragraph 7.10).

40.   The local authority's power in Scotland to impose conditions on a procession in advance should be supplemented by a statutory police power to impose conditions on the spot which will be subject to the same criteria as are proposed for England and Wales (paragraph 7.11).

41.   The police in Scotland should have the same power as in England and Wales to impose limited conditions on static demonstrations and subject to the same criteria (paragraph 7.12).

Source: *Review of Public Order Law* (Cmnd. 9510), HMSO 1985.

Appendix 2 THE NCCL'S CHARTER OF CIVIL RIGHTS AND LIBERTIES

We are committed to the defence and extension of civil liberties in the United Kingdom, and to the rights and freedoms recognised by international law. In particular, we are pledged to ensure and safeguard these essential rights:-

1. To live in freedom and safe from personal harm.
2. To protection from ill-treatment or punishment that is inhuman or degrading.
3. To equality before law and to freedom from discrimination on such grounds as disability, political or other opinion, race, religion, sex, or sexual orientation.
4. To protection from arbitrary arrest and unnecessary detention, the right to a fair, speedy and public trial, to be presumed innocent until proved guilty, and to legal advice and representation.
5. To a fair hearing before any authority exercising power over the individual.
6. To freedom of thought, conscience and belief.
7. To freedom of speech and publication.
8. To freedom of peaceful assembly and association.
9. To move freely within one's country of residence and to leave and enter it without hindrance.
10. To privacy and the right of access to official information.

Other titles of related interest

Trade Unionists: How the Public Order proposals affect you £1.50

Your right to march, to hold open-air meetings and to picket are under threat. These rights are part of the freedom to assemble peacefully, which has been won from often unwilling governments and unsympathetic courts by groups of organised workers over the centuries.

Defence of these freedoms has been one of NCCL's major tasks since it was founded in 1934. We are publishing this pamphlet to inform trade unionists of the likely effect of the Government's proposals.
NCCL 1985

Free to Walk Together £1.50

A guide to the Government's Public Order proposals for campaigning groups, voluntary organisations and church groups.
NCCL 1985

Called to Account £3.95

Sarah Spencer

This book argues for a change in the law to establish a radically different structure of police accountability, under the direction of elected representatives at local and national level. It explains clearly the powers and responsibilities of local police authorities and shows why, in practice, they are inadequate. It makes the case for a genuine tripartite structure, in which police authorities would have ultimate responsibility for police policies, priorities and operations, within a framework of minimum standards, guidelines and safeguards established by parliament.
NCCL 1985.

Police & Criminal Evidence Act 40p

Civil Liberty briefing on the Act, covering stop and search, search of premises, arrest, detention, questioning and treatment by the police, complaints and evidence.
NCCL 1985.

ADD POST AND PACKING: Total up to £1.95: 25p
Total £2.00 – £4.95: 40p
Total £5.00 – £9.95: 75p
Over £10.00: POST FREE

NCCL, 21 Tabard Street, London SE1 4LA